MAKING SENSE OF FAITH

An Introduction to Theology

MAKING SENSE OF FAITH

AN INTRODUCTION TO THEOLOGY

CHARLES HILL

E. J. DWYER

First published in 1995 by
E.J. Dwyer (Australia) Pty Ltd
Unit 13, Perry Park
33 Maddox Street
Alexandria NSW 2015
Australia
Phone: (02) 550-2355
Fax: (02) 519-3218

National Library of Australia
Cataloguing-in-Publication data
Hill, Charles, 1931– .
Making sense of faith: a introduction to theology.

Includes indexes.
Bibliography
ISBN 0 85574 150 3

1. Theology. I. Title.

230

Nihil Obstat: Richard Lennan, DTh
Imprimatur: + David Cremin, DD, VG
Sydney, May 12, 1995

The *Nihil Obstat* and *Imprimatur* are a declaration that a book is considered to be free from doctrinal and moral error. It is not necessarily implied that those who have granted them agree with the contents, opinions or statements expressed.

Cover design by Michael Killalea
Cover represents the eucharistic *Fractio panis* from the Catacombs of Priscilla, Rome, the work of an early theologian (2nd century).
Text design by Michael Killalea
Typeset in Bodoni Book by Adept Type Pty Ltd
Printed in Australia by Griffin Paperbacks, Netley, S.A.

10 9 8 7 6 5 4 3 2 1
99 98 97 96 95

Distributed in the United States by:
        Morehouse Publishing
        871 Ethan Allen Highway
        RIDGEFIELD CT 06877
        Ph: (203) 431 3927
        Fax: (203) 431 3964
        Fax: (01) 288 3700

        Distributed in Canada by:
        Meakin and Associates
        Unit 17
        81 Auriga Drive
        NEPEAN, ONT K2E 7Y5
        Ph: (613) 226 4381
        Fax: (613) 226 1687

Distributed in Ireland and the U.K. by:
        Columba Book Service
        93 The Rise
        Mount Merrion
        BLACK CO.DUBLIN
        Ph: (01) 283 2954

        Distributed in New Zealand by:
        Catholic Supplies (NZ) Ltd
        80 Adelaide Road
        WELLINGTON
        Ph: (04) 384 3665
        Fax: (04) 384 3663

To Hetty, Marie Therese and
all your sisters,
in the painful and liberating
search for understanding

I have written this little work from the viewpoint
of people trying to raise their minds to contemplate God
and seeking to understand what they believe.

(St Anselm of Canterbury, 11th century, introducing
his work on theology, *Faith Seeking Understanding*.)

I find much in these pages that is simply excellent.

Gerald O'Collins SJ, Professor of Fundamental Theology,
Gregorian University, Rome

This book is among the most comprehensive and practical Introductions to theology available. It covers the topic with an impressive thoroughness and clarity which reflect Dr Hill's experience in teaching theology. Exercises, tables, illustrations, glossary, indexes and further readings all make it user-friendly. It is ideal for anyone wishing to find out what theology today is all about.

Associate Professor Gideon Goosen,
Australian Catholic University

It is a pleasure to read a book that sincerely seeks from the outset to hold together the many disparate threads of the Eastern and Western tradition alike: the evangelical and the ecumenical, the historical and the theological, the liturgical and the cultural. This Introduction inspires and instils an open attitude of both mind and heart in those who wish to "make sense of faith."

Professor John Chryssavgis,
Holy Cross Greek Orthodox College, Boston

Karl Barth, the celebrated Swiss Calvinist, said one time that the theologian must have the Bible in one hand and the daily paper in the other. Charles Hill's book is a strikingly good example of doing just that, and urging others to do the same. The author approaches his subject from the standpoint of history, sensitive to the central truth that all 'theologizing' takes place in a determined time and place, even as Jesus himself was a man of his own day. It is as up-to-date in current events as the latest news from the troubled world, completely conversant with the latest documents of the Catholic Church, yet with a refreshing grasp of history, beginning with the Scriptures and the ancient patristic authors, of the East and West, proceeding through the medieval ups and downs of Scholasticism, into the modern period of the Reformation and its aftermath and the 'new learning,' up to the present eve of the bimillennium. There is generous use of insights not only from other Christian churches but also non-Christian testimonies. Meant to provoke critical thought, this is not a book for the comfortably complacent. Further reading recommendations are given with great attention to their availability in English.

Eamon R. Carroll, O.Carm., Emeritus Professor of Theology,
Loyola University, Chicago

Acknowledgments

For help with some of the tables, I am grateful to Mark Breheny.

CONTENTS

LIST OF TABLES

Preface

Theology is sometimes given a bad name—"a device to keep agnostics in the Church," the comic character Sir Humphrey Appleby styled it—but willy nilly we are doing it all the time. From the child's persistent questions about a God who can give us blessing and yet take Grandma from us, to the lyricist's anguished "What's it all about, Alfie?", we constantly prove our rational humanity by trying to make sense of what we believe. In other words, we are theologizing, exemplifying theology as process, bringing our brains to bear on our beliefs.

That many brains have been brought to bear on beliefs over many years is evident from the massive corpus of theological writing in print—theology as product, if you like. It is a body of theology that is ever growing; the composer of the Fourth Gospel in his time envisaged "the world itself not containing the books that would be written" (*Jn* 21.25) if we continued theologizing about Jesus alone—and we have. And not simply Christology but the Godhead, soteriology, ecclesiology and so many other branches of the multi-discipline that is theology have produced their own pile. Even before John, the theologian responsible for *Ecclesiastes* lamented, "Of making many books there is no end" (*Eccl* 12.12)—and he himself added to the pile!

To help us in our efforts to grapple with all this theological writing, theologians have written even more, supplementing lectures and classes in theological institutions. Serious students aiming at complete competence in the discipline, and even competent theologians, would be enlightened by reading a book like John Macquarrie's *Principles of Christian Theology*, an exhaustive description of philosophical, symbolic and applied theology in well over 500 pages. There is, in fact, quite a large collection of works entitled *Introduction to Theology* or some such—though many in fact introduce us rather to topics like revelation and the Trinity, which fall instead within the distinct disciplines of fundamental or systematic theology, as we shall see in due course.

Not all of us aim to become professional theologians. Some will enrol in academic institutions to pursue a complete sequence of all theological categories. Others may want simply to learn the skills and resources, concepts and idioms of theology, and thus handle better the inescapable task of theologizing about the vagaries of life and the challenges belief sets us—in other words, reach the understanding that theology offers to faith. We can then decide more securely whether formal study of the major divisions of theology is for us.

It will also prove instructive, whether we are beginners only or more serious students, by way of introduction to see how others before us have coped with this challenge of making sense of belief—belief in providence, like the author of *Ecclesiastes*; belief in Jesus, like the fourth evangelist; belief in Christianity's validity, like the Apologists and other early Fathers; belief in the whole Christian mystery, like the early framers of creeds and Council statements; belief in the equity of the divine plan, like liberationist and feminist theologians today. At these and other stages, what we are witnessing is the community theologizing, struggling to bring some understanding and reasonable expression to what faith tells them. (We are speaking of the Christian community, but other communities of course have their own theologians.) We today are not the first to face the challenge; our community has its long story and has provided some answers in the course of it.

So this Introduction to theology offers the adult beginner an insight into the skills, idioms, concepts and divisions of theology, and the resources available to the theologian, while at the same time tracing the story of the Christian community at work at this process of theologizing. To help develop these skills, each chapter closes with some exercises in doing theology. For those interested in greater depth, there are suggestions of further reading (including a gentle introduction to the many theological journals) and directions to be followed. An effort has been made to provide a text that is user-friendly; slabs of unrelieved writing may be characteristic of some theological works, but are not what the beginner requires.

In writing this text I am responding to reviewers' comments on my earlier effort at an Introduction to theology, which has gone out of print (*Faith in Search of Understanding*, Melbourne: CollinsDove, 1989). More urgently, I am able now to take account of the significant developments in that half-decade that our theology must deal with. We are not simply in the postmodern, post-Vatican II, post-cold war era, but in the wake also of the 1990 Roman Instruction on *The ecclesial vocation of the theologian*, the Seventh Assembly of the World Council of Churches in Canberra in 1991 on the theme "Come, Holy Spirit, Renew the face of the Earth," the 1992 Earth Summit at Rio, the 1992 *Catechism of the Catholic Church*, and two important Roman statements in 1993, the encyclical *Veritatis Splendor* on morality and the Pontifical Biblical Commission's Instruction *The Interpretation of the Bible in the Church*. You could think of other events challenging our theology— Gulf War, Somalian famine, Balkan conflicts, Rwandan massacres, *perestroika*. Hopefully this text will help equip us to accommodate them within an adequate theology.

1

Why do theology?

"Doing theology" is not an option for most of us. We are forced into it as rational human beings who are also believers—though we may not choose to undertake formal study of this discipline. Many a person has struggled to align belief in God with the raw deal life has given them, from Job in the Old Testament bewailing his misfortunes and even earlier in ancient writing from Egypt and Mesopotamia.

> *My strength is weakened, my prosperity has ended,*
> *Moaning and trouble have darkened my features . . .*
> *My god decreed poverty instead of wealth.*
> *A cripple does better than I.*
>
> THE BABYLONIAN THEODICY

Not all such unwitting theologians have recognized their theologizing for what it is. Often, especially when they fail to solve this particular age-old problem of retribution that worried those ancient oriental composers and countless others since, such people fall to blaming not their *theology* but *religion*. More than once have we heard from people what Australian writer A. B. Facey had to say in reflecting on his hardships. Facey turned to writing only at the end of a long and difficult life. His autobiography was entitled, perhaps with some irony, *A Fortunate Life*. He failed to reconcile it all, and particularly his experience of trench warfare, with belief in God:

> *Considering the many hundreds of different religions that*
> *there are in this world of ours, and the fact that many*
> *religions have caused terrible wars and hatreds*
> *throughout the world, and the many religions have*
> *hoarded terrific wealth and property while people inside*
> *and outside of the religion are starving, it is difficult to*
> *remain a believer. No, sir, there is no God, it is only a*
> *myth.*

FAITH, RELIGION AND THEOLOGY

Religion is the culprit in Facey's view, though a careful reading of *Job* and *The Babylonian Theodicy* might have proved helpful in focusing on these distant composers' attempts to deal with the same *theological* problem. Others since then have succeeded in seeing light where they found only darkness or resignation. For some people, on the other hand, *faith* is wrongly seen to be the problem when more properly *religion* should be in focus. How frequently do we meet anguished parents who lament the discovery that their children, on whom every attention has been showered, have "lost the faith." This usually means they have given up (for the time being) the practice of their religion. Faith, the educators tell us, may in fact simply be passing through a normal questioning phase in such youngsters, manifested by changes in religious practice.

For religion is not faith, nor is it theology—though hopefully we can presume faith in religious people and in theologians. *Religion* should be the authentic expression of belief; being human we look to discern the faith of people in their actions and are quick to detect any discrepancy. The epistle of *James* puts it bluntly:

> *If any think they are religious, and do not bridle their*
> *tongues but deceive their hearts, their religion is worthless.*
> *Religion that is pure and undefiled before God, the Father,*
> *is this: to care for orphans and widows in their distress,*
> *and to keep oneself unstained by the world* (Jas 1.26–27).

Old Testament prophets like Amos, Hosea and Jeremiah had likewise lamented the shortcomings of organized religion and religious officials by comparison with real faith: "even though you make many prayers I will not listen," the Lord says in disgust to the contemporaries of Isaiah of Jerusalem (*Is* 1.15). On the positive side we class a Mother Teresa as truly religious because her belief declares itself conspicuously in selfless behavior. Bert Facey would have been impressed—though he still had that theological problem of evil in the world to overcome, as we all do. Religion does not suffice for theology, nor does faith.

Religion, then, in being readily observable, is clearly distinct from faith and theology. *Faith*, presumed in both, is less easy to define. (The branch of study known as fundamental theology endeavors to do so more completely.) We have seen parents confusing faith with the practice of religion, especially Sunday worship. Isaiah's contemporaries tried to substitute for it a plethora of formulas. A large city newspaper recently asked a range of its readers what they meant by faith (in God, as distinct from human faith). One, a radio newsreader, replied, "It gives my life structure, it gives the world some sort of meaning." A cabinet minister: "Faith gives a sense of direction and purpose to my life." A screenwriter: "With faith you begin seeing the universe as a gigantic work of art rather than as an infinitely interesting assembly of random elements." A school principal: "I think life without faith would be a rather featureless landscape."

SAYING AMEN TO GOD

For these people faith supplies some sort of vision or meaning. The Bible sees it rather differently: Artur Weiser concludes from his study that "faith in Old Testament terms is saying Amen to God" (where the roots of the word *Amen* denote all that is reliable and trustworthy). So presumably faith in the New Testament is saying Amen to God in Jesus. In that sense we really can take things "on faith," relying utterly on God. The author of the Epistle to the Hebrews agrees: "Faith is the assurance of things hoped for, the conviction of things not seen" (11.1); and he lists biblical figures who have based their life on that conviction— Abel, Enoch, Noah, and eminently Abraham, who "set out not knowing where he was going." There is some sense of response to divine command in this, hence Paul speaks of "the obedience of faith" (*Rom* 16.26).

The medieval systematic theologians, whom we shall see at work in Chapter 7, not satisfied with a simple biblical notion of faith, psychologized it to see intellect and will separately engaged in our act of faith. "Faith is the act of the intellect assenting to divine truth under the dominion of the will as moved by God's grace" goes Thomas Aquinas's definition, which today strikes us as somewhat mechanical. The First Vatican Council was satisfied to keep the accent on intellect and truth: "Faith is a supernatural virtue whereby under the inspiration and assistance of grace we believe those things revealed by God to be true . . . because of the authority of God himself revealing."

A. B. Facey would not be content with such an accent alone, nor can we recognize it in the heroism of Mother Teresa or Vincent de Paul. A century on from Vatican I, accordingly, while dutifully gathering up all said hitherto, the Second Vatican Council inserted a key extension of faith to involve not simply intellect and will but the whole person.

Though easily overlooked, it is what *James* wrote about millennia ago:

> The "obedience of faith" must be given to God who reveals,
> an obedience by which people entrust their whole self to
> God, offering "the full submission of intellect and will to
> God who reveals," and freely assenting to the truth
> revealed by him (Constitution on Divine Revelation, #5;
> emphasis added).

So this is the wholly personal faith that informs the actions of heroes like Dorothy Day and Maximilian Kolbe and Oscar Romero and others in a list of faith-figures today parallelling that of *Hebrews*. Their faith consists not only of *confidence*, and *confession* (as Isaiah knew), but *commitment* too—totally personal commitment.

If such is faith, what need is there of theology? Certainly, to listen to Mother Teresa (as I once had the privilege of doing) one has the impression of someone conspicuously short on theologizing, proceeding rather from Gospel counsel directly to action. She said on that occasion:

> I remember one day they brought a man half of whose
> body was eaten up with cancer. He was so smelly that
> nobody could stand him. I happened to be in the house
> with him and I started washing him. And he said to me,
> "Why are you doing this?" . . . He was a Hindu man and I
> told him what Jesus had said. And I said, "I really believe I
> am touching his body in you." And then he said, "Glory to
> Jesus Christ through you!" And I said "No, but glory to
> Jesus Christ through you, because you are sharing in his
> Passion."

There's something fundamentalist about such a literal response to awful reality. What would you and I have done—theologized about it and done nothing? There are limits to theology, it is clear.

In the beatific vision, too, all that is obscure in the divine plan will be revealed; faith will not be required then, either. But, short of that experience, faith is requisite, and yet does not always suffice—otherwise we would be deprived of one Vatican Council's improvement of an earlier one's limited understanding of faith itself. For understanding is what theology brings to faith, as the title of this book suggests. Bert Facey failed to achieve it, as did the author of *Job* before him, when wrestling with an apparently vindictive God: "Why have you made me your target? Why have I become a burden to you?" (7.20).

FROM FAITH TO UNDERSTANDING

Many of the world's major religious traditions allow that it is possible and appropriate to look beyond faith for some further understanding. It has certainly been a key conviction of Christianity. "I believe; help my unbelief," cries out a distressed parent to Jesus in the Gospels, and his wish is granted (*Mk* 9.25–29). Encouraged by such expressions, Christian scholars have pondered the intricacies of biblical texts. Augustine, bishop of Hippo in north Africa, was inspired by this very passage and by the further suggestion in *Isaiah* (7.9, in the Greek version: "If you do not have faith, neither will you have understanding"). So in preaching on these texts he assured his sixth century congregation that his commentary on the scriptural Word of God could contribute something further to their faith in that Word. With the love for paradox that always fascinated him, he expresses this assurance boldly, aware also that it may seem somewhat pretentious:

> *Understand with a view to faith; have faith with a view to*
> *understanding. I will explain in a nutshell how to take*
> *this without arousing controversy: Understand my word*
> *with a view to faith, have faith in God's Word with a view*
> *to understanding* (Sermon 43).

His listeners believe the Word of God, but their faith can lead on to fuller understanding, thanks to Augustine's own commentary, which will itself deepen their faith.

This fertile interchange between faith and learning is a hallmark of Christian teaching and has prompted the accent on theological study in all its branches in the various churches. This occurs despite the unease of fundamentalists, who resist the connection between divine and human in faith development. They unconsciously resist it also in its prime analogue, the Incarnation, as we shall see in Chapter 9. An uninformed faith is at risk; the whole history of faith education in every country is testimony to this conviction on the part of believers (as we shall examine further in Chapter 13).

5

Five centuries after Augustine we get the classic definition of theology in these terms by Anselm of Canterbury. With Augustine's treatment of *Mark* 9 and *Isaiah* 7.9 in mind, he writes a little book on theology which he first entitles *Fides quaerens intellectum* (later known as *Proslogion*), "faith seeking understanding." He introduces it thus:

> *I have written this little work from the viewpoint of persons trying to raise their mind to contemplate God and seeking to understand what they believe.*

Job attempted no less in his day. The same can be said of his Mesopotamian counterparts before him, Augustine and the other Fathers we shall study in Chapter 5, the great systematic theologians in the Middle Ages, the victims and survivors of the Holocaust, Hiroshima, and the Rwandan massacres in our day. When we come to the study of theology, we come on that same basis. We are not simply *philosophizing*. "To be or not to be" could be the query of any interested inquirer into life's inequities. Faith is not posing that query.

NOT PHILOSOPHY NOR WORDINESS

Theology, then, is not to be equated with the merely reasonable arguments of philosophy, nor to be confined to the written formulations of professional theologians. Karl Rahner, one of the most conspicuous of the latter fraternity, defines theology as "the conscious and methodical explanation and explication of the divine revelation received and grasped in faith." His many erudite books on the subject certainly document that definition. But does it allow equally for the *process* of theologizing— as distinguished in our Preface from the *product*? Does this definition allow for the incipient efforts of professional and nonprofessional alike, young and old who, in Anselm's words, set about "raising their mind to God and seeking to understand what they believe"?

No, words are not essential to theology; they can in fact devalue it. I come to this page from the sad funeral of a 33-year-old suicide. Last week, under pressure of work, after a parting glimpse at his little daughter of eighteen months, he took his own life. We gathered to mourn him and comfort his wife and parents in a religious ceremony; but the plethora of words in which faith sought understanding threatened to cheapen our grief. We were left ultimately to our faith in another 33-year-old who passed through an equally awful death to a glorious life.

Yes, theology has its limits, and words are not its only coin. In our grief our eyes rested on the stained glass representation of the Risen One ascending, accompanied by All Saints, expressing as powerfully as the text from the *Book of Wisdom* the triumph over untimely death. Artists in stone and canvas have brought understanding to faith for centuries; audio and visual media continue the tradition today. From the "psalms and hymns and spiritual canticles" of Paul's communities to medieval dirges like *Stabat Mater* and *Dies Irae* to the modern reinterpretation of *Jesus Christ Superstar*, music has reflected changing responses to the mysteries of Christian faith.

All the mysteries, too. The object of theology is not simply death and pain but joy and love as well, creation and judgment, the cross and resurrection both. If the God, the *theos*, in our theo-logy is to make sense to us, the divine hand must be seen at work in all of these. Theologizing can help us discern that hand, and we should develop the habit (as Aquinas defines theology). Walter Burghardt expresses it well:

> *The world needs theologians. Yes, this absurd little earth, where a billion humans fall asleep hungry, this glorious globe that was freed from slavery by the crucifixion of its God, this paradoxical planet that nurtures love and hate, despair and hope, skepticism and faith, tears and smiles, wine and blood, this creation of divine love where men and women die for one another and kill one another—this world desperately needs theologians.*

SOME FURTHER READING

This initial chapter has endeavored to clarify the nature, purpose, scope and object of theology for beginners who may be unclear about them. We are basically not studying the nature of faith here. That would normally come later in fundamental theology, which will also go into other basic areas such as revelation. As with Introductions to theology, so fundamental theology has an abundant literature available; works by Gerald O'Collins are classic: *Fundamental Theology* (1981) and *Retrieving Fundamental Theology* (1993), New York: Paulist. Some books tend to fudge the distinction between these two types of theological preparation, which causes unnecessary confusion.

We have also made the important point that despite some popular confusion theology is not religion. There is, of course, a vast literature about religion—its nature and phenomenological manifestations—and religions in all their variety. Religions offer their adherents a meaning system, generally a way of salvation, and often rituals of worship; this offering is frequently expressed as "creed-code-cult." The scope of theology is obviously quite different. A work that endeavors to treat of faith and religion and also to perform the function of an Introduction to theology is that by B. R. Hill, P. Knitter and W. Madges, *Faith, Religion and Theology. A Contemporary Introduction*, Mystic: Twenty-Third Publications, 1990. A challenging article on the difference between religion and faith by a fine theologian is John Thornhill's "Is religion the enemy of faith?" *Theological Studies* 45 (1984), 254–274. (*Theological Studies* is one of the more sophisticated theological journals in English.)

That the niggling questions to which theology seeks an answer trouble both peasant and pope emerges from John Paul II's book *Crossing the Threshold of Hope* (Eng. trans., London: Jonathan Cape, 1994), which has chapters entitled "If God exists, why is he hiding?" and "Why is there so much evil in the world?"

Yet the scope of theology is not just the dark side of life—death and evil and suffering; the *Psalms* include equal expressions of joy and praise and thanksgiving and are thus a helpful counterbalance to *Job*. It is a pity that theology can seem problem-centered; we need someone like Mother Teresa and her heroism to provide another focus for our efforts to make sense of faith (*Something Beautiful for God* is the title of Malcolm Muggeridge's book about her). Walter Burghardt's article from which we quoted, "This world desperately needs theologians," eloquently explores theology's scope; it can be found in a less sophisticated journal, *Catholic Mind* 79 (March 1981), 33–41.

EXERCISES IN THEOLOGY

1. In the classic movie *Miracle on 34th Street,* Maureen O'Hara tries to convince young Margaret O'Brien of the reasonableness of belief in Santa Claus by urging, "Faith is believing in things when common sense tells you not to." What is your definition of Christian faith? Is it compatible with common sense, understanding, learning?

2. Over the centuries the arts have had a role to play in helping faith make sense. Name some instances that exemplify for you an influential theological role played by artists. Has the Bible movie ever successfully filled this role?

3. Letters to correspondence columns of Catholic newspapers often reflect some hostility to "theologians" as a subversive group. Why, in principle, is this to be expected? Prepare a reply to such correspondents on the necessity of theology for an informed faith.

2

Doing theology today

We can define theology as bringing understanding to faith. Augustine, we saw, was convinced he had something to contribute to his congregation's grasp of divine revelation conveyed in the Scriptures. His hundreds of sermons, not to mention all his numerous (and happily extant) other works, testify to this deep conviction of his. Theology—his and his congregation's—drew on scriptural revelation and also on his explication of those biblical texts, a skill he had developed and worked at developing in his listeners. Would that we too had been present at this master's exegesis so that we might "understand with a view to faith."

The contribution Augustine made to his congregation's faith development depended much on his own make-up, itself affected by his education and environment. He tells us in the *Confessions* that his mother Monica, solidly pious as she was, insisted that he have a good grounding in the pagan classics to make him a better Christian! A paradox here, but a soundly Christian one; and we are the richer for his rhetorical skills thus honed. What Christian theology has less cause to rejoice at in his formation are certain features of contemporary African Christianity and the manicheism with which he was associated in his youth and which left indelible marks on him—and thus on his theologizing. (Unfortunately, Christian theology, at least in the West, continued to carry those blemishes.)

THE CONTEXT OF THEOLOGY

The point is a general one: theology does not occur in a vacuum. The light of faith illumines us all as believers, yet as we theologize our reason is influenced by many other factors, even by our disposition. The dyspeptic Qoheleth who laments so often in the book of *Ecclesiastes*, "Vanity of vanities! All is vanity," could never have been responsible for the enthusiastic praise of creation that theologians like some of the psalmists and the author of *Job* give voice to. Tradition assigns to evangelist-theologians the symbols of a lion, an ox, a man (to Mark, Matthew and Luke respectively), but only "John the divine" with his distinctive theology warrants the symbol of the soaring eagle.

Likewise, as in Augustine's case, the world around us and our knowledge of and attitude towards it color our theologizing. In Chapter 5 we shall see that the Fathers of the East were much more positive and optimistic about the world and the human condition than that great scholar of the West—a good reason why we should read their theology, too. It follows that our theology today will have a different scope and character from either group of theologians in those times because we know and view the world and its inhabitants differently from them.

The whole cosmos has come into focus for us, thanks to modern cosmology and astrophysics and the technology that took us to the moon and gave us the Hubble telescope, in a way that obviously eluded the creation theologians of *Genesis*. We may concede that the biblical accounts have much to tell us about the *truth* of God's creating, but as to the *facts* they were in total ignorance—an admission that would embarrass only a fundamentalist reader of Scripture. Augustine is given credit by a modern astromathematician like Paul Davies for his acute understanding of space and time; but he would have been happy to join in Rome's angry reponse to Copernican thinking about a solar (instead of an earth-centered) system that earned Galileo his condemnation in 1633. In lifting that condemnation (in 1992!) Pope John Paul II warned theologians not to repeat the error of invoking an inadequate worldview in developing their theology:

> *It is therefore not to be excluded that one day we shall find ourselves in a similar situation, one which will require both sides to have an informed awareness of the field and the limits of their own competencies.*

That "one day" would seem to have arrived, as far as our cosmotheology goes. Our "informed awareness" must extend not simply to a heliocentric planetary system, but as well to the fact that it shares our galaxy, the Milky Way, with about a hundred billion stars. The Milky Way is but one of millions of such observable galaxies in our Universe. We must concede that what we can observe is as little as 10 per cent or even 1 per cent, the rest constituting "dark matter," in cosmologists' terms. We also need to concede, as we theologize about the world, that there is nothing special or privileged about our planetary home. It is not at the center of the Universe (as distinct from that great unseen universe), just one of billions of heavenly bodies. We know the Universe is expanding and at a rate that suggests its origins 10 or so billion years ago.

We also know more than our forebears about the cosmos. They liked to picture God related to the universe in a mechanistic way as clockmaker and repairer, thus making him responsible for all the evils in the world. Einstein's theory of relativity, acceptance of an uncertainty principle in nature, quantum physics and chaos theory have forced us to admit that events occur in nature without well-defined causes. To some extent the "real world" is created by our observing it, not vice versa. Life is possible elsewhere in this Universe, as is—mathematically speaking—the existence of other universes. Can we presume God is interested only in our welfare, on this planet, in this galaxy, in this universe? Should we in anthropocentric fashion consider only our welfare, or with a biocentric ethic look to all living things? Or even take responsibility for "all things, things in heaven and things on earth," as the letter to the Ephesians (1.10) sees the extent of the mystery of Christ? The Earth Summit in Rio in 1992 has alerted us to our total global responsibility.

A BRAVE NEW THEOLOGY

In "this brave new world" (the Shakespearean title of Aldous Huxley's futuristic novel early this century) we need a brave new theology. Thomas Aquinas supplies us with a helpful model of adapting theology by accommodating faith to newer understandings. In the thirteenth century he made use of recently available Greek and Arabic philosophy to develop a more adequate theological system. This allowed him to do greater justice to the totality of the Christian mystery, as we shall see in Chapter 7. At the time though he was officially condemned for thus being too rationalistic in method and naturalistic in attitude. Later his *Summa* came to be accepted as providing the model of theological completeness—until, in our time, our greater access to and understanding of Scripture led to other models being suggested.

It will be ever thus. The Incarnation demands that theologians respond to the advances in human sciences just as they do to greater depthing of their understanding of the sources of revelation. Pope John Paul II said as much above in pastoral vein. Before him Augustine in his *De Doctrina Christiana* gave a theological basis for this adaptation to human progress:

> *Everything could well have been done by an angel; but the*
> *standing of the human race would have been devalued if*
> *God had seemed unwilling to let people act as the agents*
> *of his Word to people.*

Today, too, we know so much more than the Bible, Augustine and Aquinas about other peoples and their religions. Though the great Asian religions of Hinduism and Buddhism had developed a decisive opening to the transcendent half a millennium before Jesus, you would never guess it from the New Testament. In Paul's theology there is only Judaism in its unreformed version and "The Way" Jews were encouraged to follow it by Jesus, to which Gentiles too were invited; otherwise nothing of any religious value. Augustine with a like ignorance could be frighteningly dogmatic on the fate of anyone not following Jesus: "Neither those who have never heard the Gospel nor those who by reason of their infancy were unable to believe . . . are separated from that mass which will certainly be damned." To Aquinas with his similarly foreshortened view of the inhabited world, religions were not worth a place in his comprehensive system; "religion" under any guise gains a place only as a moral virtue.

And yet (at least) in Asia and Australia people had been experiencing and expressing in noble form their relationship with the divine for tens of thousands of years, as we now know and admire. The Pope in speaking to Aborigines in Alice Springs in 1986 affirmed the depth of their ancient spirituality:

> *For thousands of years you have lived in this land and*
> *fashioned a culture that endures to this day. And during*
> *all this time, the Spirit of God has been with you. Your*
> *"Dreaming," which influences your lives so strongly that,*
> *no matter what happens, you remain for ever a people of*
> *your culture, is your own way of touching the mystery of*
> *God's Spirit in you and in creation. You must keep your*
> *striving for God and hold on to it in your lives.*

THE THEOLOGY OF A MINORITY

In our contemporary theologizing about these people and their ancient religions we must move beyond the horizons of Augustine and even Paul, if only because we cannot plead the ignorance limiting their vision. After two millennia of Christianity, in today's world of well over five billion people only one third (and a diminishing third at that) acknowledge Jesus as lord and savior. The vast bulk of people belong to other religions and look to them for their way of salvation. What has our theology to say in response to these statistics? Ignore the existence of the non-Christian majority, like the Bible generally? Condemn them all to perdition, like Augustine and a long history of Christian teaching before and after his time? Look for the positive salvific qualities of these other religions, in the manner of Vatican II's statement on them?

Doing theology today means taking account of these aspects of today's world. Salvation is its "fundamental, central and even crucial theological problem," Edward Schillebeeckx tells us. And salvation has a cosmic, ecological dimension as well, as the Rio summit and conservationists (and Wisdom and Paul before them) point out. A meeting of UNESCO was told some years ago by an Indian delegate, "If we work for the poor and the penguins simultaneously, we can hope for a better present and future."

Fortunately, theology is not the preserve of Christian churchmen. At least from the sages of ancient Egypt and Mesopotamia, and the rabbis of restored Israel, faith in God has been accompanied by efforts to find understanding of the world's problems—and this is true also of the other great religions and the scientific community. As theologians our reading should include not just the Bible but the Koran, the Vedas and Upanishads of Hinduism, the Tripitaka of Buddhism, the Zoroastrian Avesta, and the works of the scientific popularizers like Paul Davies, Stephen Hawking, Charles Birch, John Gribbin. To do justice to a creative God, who is the *theos* of our theology, like the psalmist we should admit that the heavens themselves proclaim his glory and invite our meditation (*Pss* 8;19). Like Amos in the eighth century before even Jesus' universalism, we should recognize the Lord's dealings with all peoples:

Are you not like the Ethiopians to me,
  O people of Israel? says the Lord.
Did I not bring Israel up from the land of Egypt,
  and the Philistines from Caphtor,
  and the Arameans from Kir? (9.7)

Doing theology today presumes in the theologian a like universalism to Jesus', who dwelt not overly on the religious institutions and practices of one people, his own, but addressed his invitation into God's kingdom to all peoples, and was content to direct his listeners to consider the birds of the air and flowers of the field as well. We are in a position to make our response in faith and theology with the advantage of an immeasurably greater appreciation of the extent of these peoples and of a cosmos that stretches well beyond the wildest dreams of his contemporaries.

The obverse of that advantage, of course, is that our theology is challenged by all the difficult issues which today's technology does not allow us to ignore: scarcity of resources, environmental pollution, destruction of the forests, acid rain, greenhouse effect, the hole in the ozone layer, global warming. And beyond these ecological challenges to our theology there are other human and moral ones: population explosion, mass unemployment, international debt crisis, unequal distribution of wealth, drug abuse, genetic engineering, discrimination against racial and religious minorities . . .

To be a theologian today is not for the fainthearted.

SOME FURTHER READING

This chapter has made a general point, that good theology is not done in a vacuum. The image of the theologian at his desk, cut off from the real world, is probably not current and certainly is not the ideal for authentic theologizing. As faith is a response to God's dealings with us in our daily life as also in the community's foundational events (like Exodus and Paschal Mystery), so theology has to make sense of that contextualized faith. We shall develop the point more fully in Chapter 12 on "Theology and theologies." I have expanded some of the relevant ideas in an article "A brave new theology," *Compass Theology Review* 27 (1993 No. 4), 1–5.

We are blessed these days with an abundance of well-communicated information from the scientific community, and in particular the cosmologists, astronomers, physicists and mathematicians, on the nature of the universe (or at least the observable Universe: the uppercase is deliberate). That is all to the good, as so much is happening by way of exploration and discovery in space beyond our atmosphere. The Discovery missions and shots from the repaired Hubble telescope, not to mention spatial happenings like meteoric collisions, make for compulsive TV viewing—and pose challenges to the theologian. Thanks, then, to the great scientific popularizers and theorists—theologians in some cases, like Charles Birch—who provide us with theological fodder about the origins, nature and future of creation.

The Mind of God is the intriguing title of a book by astromathematician Paul Davies (borrowed from the final sentence of another, perhaps less accessible, work by a great contemporary mathematician, Stephen Hawking, *A Brief History of Time*). Davies writes: "Through my scientific work I have come to believe more and more strongly that the physical universe is put together with an ingenuity so astonishing that I cannot accept it merely as brute fact. There must, it seems to me, be a deeper level of explanation. Whether one wishes to call that deeper level 'God' is a matter of taste and definition" (16). Davies himself "does not subscribe to a conventional religion"—but he certainly stimulates theologians in their theologizing about this marvelous world.

We live in a multi-faith world, and most of us in multi-faith communities. Our attitude to these different religions, since Paul and Augustine, is thankfully more positive—even if in my own country we have been slow to acknowledge the spiritual riches of a people in residence here well over forty millennia before the rest of us arrived. It is difficult to stand with a foot in more than one religious community and thus soundly theologize about this multi-faith world. Someone who spent much of his life in this endeavor was Dom Bede Griffiths, English convert and Benedictine, and later apologist for Asian religions from his ashram in India. We are indebted to him for this universal viewpoint, expressed in works like *A New Vision of Reality. Western Science, Eastern Mysticism and Christian Faith* (1990), London: Fount, 1992. The Catholic community's more positive assessment of other religions received decisive formulation in Vatican II's *Declaration on the Relationship of the Church to Non-Christian Religions* in 1965.

EXERCISES IN THEOLOGY

1. Galileo was condemned by the theologians of his time through their lack of "informed awareness," in Pope John Paul II's words. List the factors that today's theologians need to take into account to avoid repeating this error of an unbalanced theology of the cosmos.
2. As Christians we believe and theologize as a minority community. What are the implications of the world's religious situation for our theologizing, in your view?
3. If you were writing a theology of salvation today, how widely would you set your horizons, knowing what you know of the world, its peoples, the risks facing both, the deliverance needed?

3

Doing theology yesterday

We reminded ourselves in the previous chapter that theology is not done in a vacuum. It is a human process, even if conducted also in the light of faith. It is therefore susceptible to influences that make us what we are. At the ceremony commemorating an untimely death mentioned in Chapter 1, the young widow bravely read Gerard Manley Hopkins' tortured poem "Carrion comfort". It movingly expresses the poet's unnamed suffering, and evidently resonated with this sufferer's grief—reducing us to tears, in fact. Death was no welcome release in this light, but took on all its injustice and cruelty. Not the time to echo Paul's willing acceptance (*Phil* 1.23).

THEOLOGY IN THE MAKING

Our theology can take on a longer perspective, however, and reveal its indebtedness to all those who in our community have sought to bring understanding to faith from the beginning. The challenges of the immediate context are in these cases different, and believers have responded differently—even in error, we might concede. A classic case of such "theology in the making" can be seen in the continuing series of attempts by sages in our tradition and others to come to grips with that very problem of suffering and injustice which has plagued us from the beginning, and clearly confronts us still. Theology, even if far more enlightened now than for the author of *The Babyonian Theodicy* three millennia ago, does not diminish the anguish of reality.

It is proverbial to cite the book of *Job* in this connection. On the day of our recent bereavement I found it unhelpful to have the minister quote at me the serene words of the uncomplaining hero of the prose prologue to that marvelous book, "The Lord gave, and the Lord has taken away; blessed be the name of the Lord" (1.21). I suppose not all present would have brought to their mourning, as I did, the handicap of holding that the book as a whole does not subscribe to the resigned sentiments of the folk hero. It is the furiously resentful Job of the long verse dialogue, set within the older prose framework, who represents the true focus of the author's interest. In reading this book—which has been called "the supreme achievement of Hebrew Wisdom," "arguably the greatest achievement of all biblical poetry" and many other superlatives—we are in fact witnessing a critical movement in theological history. The preacher that day, in dispensing to us simply the traditional piety of the idealized sufferer of the folktale, was unconsciously belittling the pain of grief, which not only the book as a whole but the grieving widow and Hopkins both refused to have dismissed.

You recall the structure of *Job* as it stands, now (in my view) a composite. In the well-known folktale (*Ezekiel* 14.14, for instance, refers to it) a good man is allowed capriciously by God, to prove a point to his loyal opposition "Satan", to undergo a series of sufferings and deprivations. Despite the urgings of his quite naturally resentful wife, Job refuses to "curse God;" and finally at the end of the book, again in prose, all his goods—property, children, health, long life—are restored. ("Mrs Job" is missing at the finale, as she is all through the verse; a later extrabiblical Jewish or Christian work *The Testament of Job* tries to give her equal billing.) The moral is clear: the Lord will see to it that good people will be rewarded for goodness in good time. There are plenty of traces of this theology in Wisdom books, especially parts of *Proverbs*, *Ecclesiastes* and *Sirach* (*Ecclesiasticus*), other books of the Old and New Testaments, and much Christian writing and preaching since—including the recent obsequies.

Intuitively Hopkins and the widow that day knew that such pat responses to deep human tragedy do not suffice. And the author of the whole book of *Job* knew it too. The theology of previous sages and traditional formulas would not do; the immensity of human suffering gives the lie to it in reality. So the Job of Chapter 3 of the book, the beginning of the verse dialogue which the author has composed to give a whole new treatment of the ancient problem, falls to cursing from the outset:

> *After this Job opened his mouth and cursed the day of his birth. Job said:*
>> *"Let the day perish in which I was born,*
>>> *and the night that said,*
>>>> *'A man-child is conceived.'*
>> *Let that day be darkness!*

May God above not seek it,
   or light shine on it.
Let gloom and deep darkness claim it."

Whatever happened to the piously resigned folk hero blessing the name
of the Lord, like our preacher that day? He is gone, our author is saying,
along with his discredited theology: it could not measure up to reality,
as piosity never can.

And the book continues in that vein. Three friends emerge, trotting
out the old lame theology that equates reward with goodness and
suffering with guilt, and lecturing Job at length on this theme. To this
Job has simply to say: Look at the facts; the Mr Bigs of this world do
very well, thank you.

The tents of robbers are at peace,
   and those who provoke God are secure (12.6).

Theology will never be the same again. This great theologian—
anonymous, like the bulk of biblical authors—has forced his peers to
ditch a patently inadequate response to real life in the light of faith.
The wisdom of the community's wise, the sages, was not keeping pace
with what they knew of the world—as the Pope warned our generation's
theologians, confronted with an explosion of knowledge, lest they be
tempted to fall back to a response akin to the sentence on Galileo.

A THEOLOGICAL BREAKTHROUGH

All credit to this great theologian for making a great "breakthrough," if
that is what it takes to get people to face reality and grapple theologically
with it. So what is his answer to the injustices of life: can the ledger be
balanced short of the grave? Remember, despite Handel, these biblical
authors had little inkling of life after death (that celebrated passage,
"In my flesh I shall see God," 19.25–27, is textually corrupt). No, while
negatively the author can show the inadequacy of a previous theology,
on the positive side he is limited by his own foreshortened theological
vision, which does not extend beyond the grave. What he can do is to
situate the human predicament within a faithfilled confidence in divine
care for the whole universe—"the Wisdom hidden in the mysterious
design of the cosmos" as distinct from the "the wisdom which mortals

21

seek so as to understand that design" (Norman Habel). So, while the book does not yet enjoy a horizon stretching to resurrection in a New Testament perspective, it does accentuate a God who is caring for history and cosmos in the round. We are chided by Job's God for not acknowledging this sooner.

> *Who has the wisdom to number the clouds?*
>   *Or who can tilt the waterskins of the heavens,*
> *when the dust runs into a mass*
>   *and the clods cling together? (38.37–38)*

It is a pity that such noble theological insight is overlooked or distorted in situations, like tragic grief, which it directly and compassionately addresses. The theology of biblical authors and the Church Fathers, yesterday's theologians admittedly, is often unappreciated by their descendants. We have to settle for the pedestrian sentiments of today's sages, as in the panegyric referred to. Partly this is due, beyond mere ignorance, to our viewing the biblical composers as historians or spokesmen (women not being to the fore) or biographers, and not primarily as theologians—or "prophets," to use a term from the Hebrew Bible.

HISTORICAL COMMENTARY AS THEOLOGY

When the Hebrew Bible arranges its material, though it tells a lot of stories which many of us read as "Bible history," there is no mention of history or story. What the Christian Bible, inadequately, calls The Historical Books—*Joshua, Judges, Samuel, Kings*—appear instead as The Former Prophets. It is no unvarnished narrative we are getting; rather, it is a commentary on past and present akin to those other, "Latter," Prophets we are more accustomed to recognizing as prophetic—Isaiah, Jeremiah, Ezekiel, The Twelve. Even with these latter we tend to misread "prophetic" to mean "foretelling the future," though the Hebrew *nabi* can mean "spokesman, commentator" (rather like our "theologian"), and that is generally the role they discharge.

So if we were to read the Prophets, Former or Latter, for the unfiltered facts of history, we would be mistaking their purpose; fundamentalists do it all the time, of course. The accent falls not on *fact* but on *truth*, a vital distinction. (Actually, our historians of note practice something similar, as much interpreting as merely recording.) It is important for us to recognize the theological approach to history adopted by these Old Testament authors, if only because the facts recorded are not always edifying. Take the "ethnic cleansing" recounted in *Joshua*. Though modern archaeologists have not been able to support the picture given there of a total invasion and displacement of the Canaanite population by the Israelites under Joshua, the book is insistent that it was necessary to preserve Israel's identity and apartness, on divine guarantee:

> *All the spoil of these towns, and the livestock, the Israelites took for their booty; but all the people they struck down with the edge of the sword, until they had destroyed them, and they did not leave anyone who breathed. As the Lord had commanded his servant Moses, so Moses commanded Joshua, and so Joshua did; he left nothing undone of all that the Lord had commanded Moses . . . For it was the Lord's doing to harden their hearts so that they would come against Israel in battle, in order that they might be utterly destroyed, and might receive no mercy, but be exterminated, just as the Lord had commanded Moses (11.14–15, 20).*

Hopefully the Bible moviemakers will not turn their hands to this; its cinematographic possibilities are awesome! But this is not cinematography: this is theology, believe it or not. *Joshua* commentator Michael Coogan remarks of these verses: "With a rhetorical flourish the authors of *Joshua* conclude their account of the conquest by reaffirming one of their major themes: Joshua's total fidelity to the divinely instituted Mosaic law (see *Deuteronomy* 20.16–17)." So to gain a clue as to the theology of these "historians" we turn to that text of *Dt*, where the Lord is speaking to Moses:

> *You shall annihilate them . . . just as the Lord your God has commanded, so that they may not teach you to do all the abhorrent things that they do for their gods, and you thus sin against the Lord your God.*

There lies the clue to the book's account of ethnic cleansing. It is less a *factual* account of what occurred (remember the archaeologists' skepticism) than the theological *truth* about Israel's need for

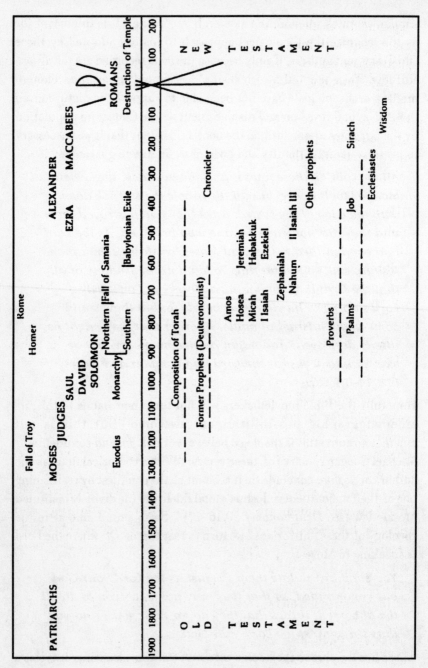

Composition of the Bible
A timeline of key figures, events, authors

"apartheid", an element of holiness in the biblical sense. In brief, you cannot mix with impiety without contracting it, so keep away (Jewish ghettos have reflected that sentiment equally starkly).

Unfortunately, we tend to read "prophecy" as "history" because (perhaps conditioned by modern information recall) we look for *fact* where *truth* instead is the intent of the composer/prophet/theologian. And, of course, preachers, politicians and warmongers in our day, misunderstanding these theologians of yesterday, have preached insipid sentiment instead of true wisdom, erected *apartheid* into political systems claiming biblical support and practiced ethnic cleansing in frightening reality. What we need to keep constantly in mind is that the biblical authors, and specifically in this case the prophetic composers of the so-called "historical books," were doing their theologizing many centuries after the events (see table, "Composition of the Bible") and had contemporary developments on their minds in reading a message from the events for their fellow Jews. Like the creation stories in *Genesis*, they were writing theology, not factual record.

So, as theologians, we take our place in a long line within the Judeo-Christian tradition at least, reaching back to the paradigmatic sage Solomon, who "was wiser than anyone else . . . and composed three thousand proverbs" (*1 Kgs* 4.31–32), to his contemporary the Yahwist, responsible for the great themes of Israel's beginnings, to the sages and prophets before and during the Exile, to the Deuteronomistic school of theologians reviewing Israel's story from the vantage point of pending disaster and highlighting the need for fidelity and even (as we have seen) apartness. The psalmists, too, with a theology for praise and thanksgiving, lament and petition; the Chronicler, throwing up in positive light the Davidic monarchy as a model of the community returned from Exile in foreign parts. Our forebears as theologians are the rabbis from the time of Ezra, commenting ceaselessly on the Torah and submitting all the TaNaK to midrashic reworking, and eventually codifying mishnah and midrashim in the Talmud, a rabbinic summa.

If we think we come to theology in isolation, in a vacuum, we deceive ourselves. Pious platitudes and justification of apartheid and ethnic cleansing are the risks we take if we ignore yesterday's theologians.

25

Some Further Reading

For Christian theologians a proper understanding of the Christian community's traditions is essential—and yet is not always part of the equipment of some of the most notable of them. Augustine did not have a knowledge of the biblical languages, nor did the vast majority of the other Fathers, nor Aquinas. Further, they generally read the biblical accounts in a literalistic fashion. For instance the story of the Fall gave rise to a theology (and then dogma) of original sin that owes much to these great but limited theologians' unsophisticated biblical science. Theologian Neil Ormerod traces this particular dogma to such (inadequate) theological roots in his *Grace and Disgrace*, Sydney: Dwyer, 1992, 99–117. It is good for us to be aware, too, of the cosmology of the biblical authors/theologians by comparison with our own.

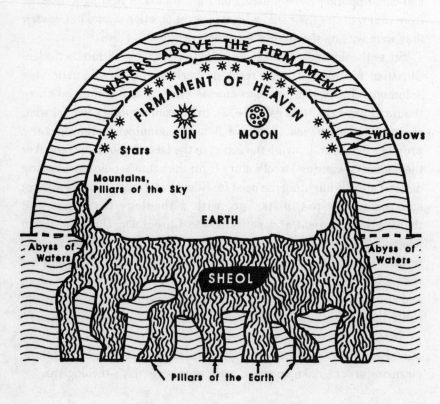

Hebrew concept of the universe

It is helpful, therefore, but rare enough to find in an Introduction to theology a treatment of the true character of the scriptural traditions of Christianity, including the Hebrew Bible. David Brown's *Invitation to Theology*, Oxford: Blackwell, 1989, has a useful chapter on yesterday's theologians entitled "The Bible's Theologians," as should all Introductions. It touches on some relevant issues: "History or theology?", "Prophets, not predicters," "Wisdom's natural theology," all of which we have raised in this chapter. I have tried in my Guide to the Old Testament (*The Scriptures Jesus Knew*, Sydney: Dwyer, 1994) to present the authors as primarily theologians and to harp on that distinction in their focus—on *truth*, not on *fact*. It remains for us as theologians to be equally critical—that is, discerning—in our use of our community's other traditions, such as liturgical and doctrinal traditions.

For this is the approach adopted these days in critical studies of the Bible. Our enhanced appreciation of biblical composition and biblical inspiration has resulted in a heightened emphasis on the contribution of the authors beyond the mere recording of fact. In the following chapter we shall see that to be true also of the Gospel composers, whom we shall style evangelist-theologians. But, in the case of the Old Testament, the great editor-composers, like the Yahwist (responsible for one great version of primeval and patriarchal traditions in *Genesis* and further into the Torah), the Deuteronomist and the Chronicler are now credited with deliberate theological reshaping of earlier traditions instead of mere record. We are indebted for this appreciation to the great German literary/theological critics, like Gerhard Von Rad in his landmark commentaries on *Genesis* and *Deuteronomy*. Antony Campbell's *The Study Companion to Old Testament Literature*, Wilmington: Glazier, 1989, continues this approach, especially in regard to the Deuteronomist.

A helpful article on historical composition generally in the ancient world is that by R. K. Gnuse, "Holy history in the Hebrew Scriptures in the ancient world" in one of the more accessible biblical journals, *Biblical Theology Bulletin* 17 (1987 No.4), 127–36.

Another area where theology—moral theology in this case—stands to benefit from critical use of the Old Testament is the Decalogue. Two recent Catholic statements, the encyclical *Veritatis Splendor* on moral matters and the *Catechism of the Catholic Church*, give great attention to the Decalogue. Moral theologians would need to be in touch with the findings of biblical studies on the character of the several Old Testament passages where this moral code in ten-point form is transmitted to us (not simply in *Exodus* and *Deuteronomy* but also in the *Psalms* and the Latter Prophets), looking at the time of composition of the text and the composer's purpose. Otherwise, there is danger of the literalism we have noted in the case of Augustine and Aquinas. David Brown in his *Invitation to Theology* looks at the issue of "Moses' enlarged role."

EXERCISES IN THEOLOGY

1. Can you recall situations where a preacher or teacher or writer has—perhaps to your irritation—failed to respect the true theological depth of the Jewish and Christian Scriptures? Locate the passage(s), and bring out the theology thus distorted.

2 On the other hand, can you nominate theological positions in the Bible which we find it necessary to refine or even jettison today? Does the Bible itself elsewhere also supply the necessary corrective?

3. Are there instances today in religious education, preaching, common usage where the attitude to the Bible's "historical" material is not sufficiently sophisticated, with the result that theology is neglected? Does the distinction between truth and fact help in dealing with this material (choose particular examples)?

Making sense of Jesus

Humility is an appropriate virtue for a theologian. We are not the first who have sought to bring understanding to faith. That we can achieve it to some extent is due in no small way to the efforts of our predecessors, yesterday's theologians, at least within our own tradition. We may now be able to fit the missing piece into the puzzle that beset the author of *Job*, and unlike him truly confess that "in my flesh I shall see God." But he had first to dispose of the superficially appealing, though basically flawed, platitudes of sages promising justice for the oppressed and grieving here and now—sentiments still to be heard, we have noted. Only then could the larger questions be posed: if not relief now, when? If not now, why me?

Nevertheless, the coming of Jesus meant an utter transformation of the theological horizon. Not only did the problem of suffering and injustice receive its potentially definitive response in the person of this innocent sufferer, who moreover lives again to promise us life with him beyond the grave. Ethnic cleansing in the name of racial and religious purity upheld by the Deuteronomist, great theological commentator though he was, also fell before the invitation addressed by Jesus to all peoples to accept the values of God's kingdom. The charter of the Sermon on the Mount dismissed all such discrimination, and proposed ideals for making all human beings truly human.

THE OBSTACLE THAT IS JESUS

And yet, of course, as we have to admit, Christian theology is the theology of a minority. Jesus, his teaching, his death and resurrection are not Good News for the bulk of our contemporaries, as they were not for his. A bishop speaking recently to an audience of Jews and Christians on the occasion of the launching of Catholic guidelines for relations between the two communities felt he had to admit,

> *Between Judaism and Christianity there stand many barriers. The greatest of all is the mountain of Jesus of Nazareth . . . It will long stand.*

To many present the bishop's words seemed a little imprudent, insensitive, unnecessarily honest, especially as he proceeded to insist that "Jesus intended to transform the symbols of Judaism and to give its tradition a new direction." The bishop in question had the advantage of his reputation for a commitment to ecumenism and inter-faith relations and also for biblical expertise. He knew well that the theologians among Jesus' own followers felt they had to grapple with "the mountain of Jesus of Nazareth" in explaining him to his contemporaries. That basically is what the New Testament is—the theologizing of a series of commentators ("prophets" in the biblical sense as we have seen) on this member of Judaism who offered as a universal variant of it "The Way" for all people, Jew and Gentile alike. The Way (cf *Acts* 9.2), incidentally, solved the enigma of the righteous sufferer posed in the Jewish Scriptures by *Job*, some psalms, the Suffering Servant of *Second Isaiah*.

As the bishop had his credentials for authentic interpretation of inter-faith problems, so too did the New Testament theologians, and principal among them their Jewishness. They spoke on Jesus from within their tradition and his. They were aware that those issues of discrimination and undeserved suffering called for solution in traditional thinking. And they present Jesus, in the line of Job and the Suffering Servant, as exemplifying particularly the righteous sufferer. In fact, that emphasis becomes the touchstone for what is orthodox in the new community, a filter for sifting out heterodox theologizing about him, as we shall see.

"OF FIRST IMPORTANCE"

It was the Pharisee Paul who, though not a companion of Jesus, was through force of circumstances the first to spell out in scriptural form the characteristic theology. After his conversion experience of the Risen Lord, he was briefed by Peter (*Gal* 1.18), doubtless on the experiences of Jesus that those earlier disciples had enjoyed. Paul brought to the task of introducing Jesus to others his own education and solid grounding in Jewish tradition. His theologizing about Jesus incorporated this common background that both inherited and the young community's story passed on from Peter and others. By the time he came as an experienced missioner to write to the local church in Corinth two decades after his conversion, he had arrived at an inflexible emphasis on the essentials of faith in Jesus, his own and the community's.

*I would remind you, brothers and sisters, of the good news
that I proclaimed to you,*
    which in turn you received,
    in which also you stand,
    through which you are being saved,
if you hold firmly to the message that I proclaimed to you
—unless you have come to believe in vain.

*For I handed on to you as of first importance
what I in turn had received:*
    that Christ died for our sins
        in accordance with the Scriptures,
        and that he was buried,
    and that he was raised *on the third day*
        in accordance with the Scriptures,
        and that he appeared . . . (1 Cor 15.1–5, emphasis
        and verse form added).

Like the creeds we perhaps (unfortunately) know better, as we shall see in Chapter 6, Paul is reciting for the Corinthian community—who were perhaps soft on the importance of the body for Jesus and themselves—a basic credal statement on Jesus. (The text goes on to talk of bodily resurrection, Jesus' and our own, you remember.) Like all credal statements, it is not a spontaneous utterance but a deliberately theologized formula; the carefully crafted rhetorical structure (which I have clarified by verse form) suggests as much. As well Paul admits by adopting the technical terms of tradition, transmission—"received," "handed on"—that it is not he but the community who have agreed on what is "of first importance."

A PASCHAL THEOLOGY

And what is that, the considered/pondered/theologized faith of the community? *Jesus died . . . Jesus rose:* all else may be forgotten if need be, but that is basic. No mention here, or elsewhere in Paul, of birth stories, parables, miracle stories, sermons of Jesus: they are not "of first importance," evidently. It is clearly a Paschal theology (Hebrew *Pesach*, "Passover"); the Easter event surpasses all others in its significance for faith.

At last the final piece of the puzzle of suffering and injustice falls into place. At last the true identity of the Royal Sufferer and the Suffering Servant of Jewish tradition is revealed. Jesus may come as a mountain for many fellow Jews, but for believers in him he removes the obstacles and the the blindfold that had impeded earlier theologians. It is a vital theological emphasis by the community, whose liturgy will similarly peak at Easter in celebrating this "Paschal Mystery,"—that is, Passover story, because it brings us too from slavery to freedom. (Christian devotion may sometimes veer from this basic focus—for instance, by dwelling more fondly on Christmas birth stories; education should correct this deviation.)

As a community's credal statement, what Paul is giving us here in *1 Corinthians* is not simply his personal theologizing but a theological emphasis arising from and contributing to the faith of the community— a typical case of Augustine's vision of the interrelationship of faith and theology. Of all that Jesus said and did, the Corinthians are to see the Paschal Mystery as basic. So, not surprisingly the Gospels, coming some decades after Paul's letter, reflect in their structure the same preoccupation with death and resurrection, though in their greater length allowing space for other mysteries of Jesus' life.

EVANGELIST-THEOLOGIANS

For the evangelists too are theologians primarily—like Paul and also like the Former Prophets of the Jewish Scriptures. Like the Deuteronomist, who is not interested in an unvarnished account of the life of Joshua or David but interprets it so as to bring out his theological message, so Matthew, Mark, Luke and John (and the many theologians to whom they are indebted: cf *Lk* 1.1–2) do not present Jesus as simple biographers. Within the same overall *structure* (see Exercise 2 following), each gives an individual portrait, in line with his individual *theology*, so that it could be said we receive in their Gospels four different Jesuses (at least). Hence the attribution to them of those four different symbols (based on Ezekiel's vision)—ox, lion, man and soaring eagle. Devotion leads us to prefer one Gospel to another, though our more theologically rigorous liturgy ensures that we get regular doses of each, to sample the Spirit at work in all four. The Pontifical Biblical Commission's

Instruction on the Gospels insists that each evangelist-theologian felt free to shape his subject:

> *Each of them followed a method suitable to the purpose which he had in view. They selected certain things out of the many which had been handed on; some they synthesized, some they explained with an eye to the situation of the churches . . . The evangelists, in handing on the words or the deeds of our Savior, explained them for the advantage of their readers by respectively setting them, one evangelist in one context, another in another.*
>
> SANCTA MATER ECCLESIA (1964)

Yet, despite all the individuality of these theologians in constructing their Gospel accounts of Jesus, when they come to recount his Passion all liberty and structural diversity disappears. Instead, there is rigid adherence of all four to what is clearly a preformed pattern in this single long narrative, by contrast with many short episodes elsewhere. Clearly, with the Passion, something "of first importance" has been reached, as the community taught Paul also. No evangelist may tamper with its principal features; Mark sets the style in a Gospel that has been called "a Passion narrative with an introduction" (Martin Kähler, 1896). Hence we may speak (as commentators like C. H. Dodd and R. E. Brown do) of the acts and scenes of a great drama in which Jesus' Passover is presented:

The Passion of Jesus
A Drama in five acts

Act I   The Leave-taking

Act II   The Arrest

Act III The Trial

          Scene 1 Examination before the High Priest

          Scene 2 Trial before the Roman governor

Act IV The Execution

Act V   The Reunion

          Scene 1 The burial

          Scene 2 The discovery of the empty tomb

          Scene 3 The appearance of the risen Christ

All evangelists reproduce *all* acts and *all* scenes (and some key details within them) in the *same* order—a remarkable and unique instance in ancient literature of convergence by different portraits on the subject's denouement.

MAKING SENSE OF SUFFERING

Again the community's faith prevails, to which individual theologies defer. Conversely, four individual theologies reinforce the community's faith, in the manner seen in Paul and in the liturgy (and, hopefully, in our devotion, in the community's dogma and catechesis). It is the vital relationship between the two—faith and theology—that Augustine and Anselm will later articulate. The integral place of Act V in the whole drama of his Passion not only makes sense of Jesus, and fits the final piece in that puzzle facing *The Babylonian Theodicy*, Israel's sages and eventually *Job*. It also makes sense of the tragic death of our 33-year-old and of all our deaths.

As often happens in a community, not all members concur in interpreting persons and events. Clearly, Jesus was and is not accepted by all his fellow Jews. And even within the ranks of his followers, there were those who were in disagreement with the way of making sense of Jesus offered by Paul and the four Gospels. Paul's lecture to the Corinthians suggests as much; they needed to be told that what befalls our bodies and Jesus' is important for faith. Then there is "The Fifth Gospel," as *The Gospel of Thomas* is being referred to by some these days. It is a composition of a gnostic group of the early century or two, so-called because of their interest more in special knowledge, *gnosis*, than in material, incarnational realities. So what distinguishes this document, composed of 114 sayings of Jesus (some perhaps as ancient as the evangelists' version), is that it is nothing more than sayings—no Paschal Mystery, so clearly vital to Paul and the evangelists for making sense of Jesus. A Jesus who does not suffer and die and rise is not "of first importance" to them and us, nor does he fit the final piece into Job's puzzle or succeed the Royal Sufferer and Suffering Servant.

Nor does he help me mourn my friend and look for his rising.

SOME FURTHER READING

As with the Old Testament, so the theological contribution of New Testament composers has benefited from advances in biblical criticism (as we shall see in greater detail in Chapter 9). In particular, *form criticism*, which studies the occurrence in biblical texts of preexisting literary units, such as the credal statement we found Paul invoking in *1 Cor*, and *redaction criticism*, which focuses upon an author's use of material to highlight his underlying theology, such as an evangelist's employment of stories from the life of Jesus, have enabled us to recognize these early theologians at work. So there is an abundance of scholarly literature highlighting their efforts to make sense of Jesus. Within the series *Biblical Foundations in Theology*, for example, a biblical scholar and a systematic theologian have combined to write *New Testament Theology in Dialogue* (London: SPCK, 1987): James Dunn and James Mackey respectively. Beyond looking at particular NT passages, they distinguish the two disciplines, aiming "to bridge the gap."

As mentioned above, it is a century since Martin Kähler in a book entitled (in its English translation) *The So-called Historical Jesus and the Historic Biblical Christ* described Mark's Gospel as "a Passion narrative with an introduction," emphasizing the predominant place given by the evangelist to this culmination of Jesus' life. For a while, with the tendency to write and read lives of Jesus, often constructed in parallel with other simple biographies, the peculiar structure of the Gospels was obscured, namely:

- preparation of Jesus for his ministry
- Jesus' ministry, largely in Galilee
- movement to Jerusalem and brief Jerusalem ministry
- PASCHAL MYSTERY.

This structure, if nothing else, distinguishes the (canonical) Gospels from mere biographies. Underlying the structure is a theology, a meditation on Jesus' life and its significance for us, which has given rise to an emphasis that is now basic to Christian faith—namely, Jesus' dying and rising.

So biblical scholars, leaving well behind those pious "lives of Jesus," have emphasized the Gospels' paschal character. The Five-Act Drama presented earlier arises from a study by C. H. Dodd, *Historical Tradition in the Fourth Gospel*, Cambridge: CUP, 1963. Since then there have been a series of studies of the Gospel Passion narratives, culminating in the monumental two volumes by Raymond E. Brown, *The Death of the Messiah*, New York: Doubleday, 1994 (parallel to his earlier equally definitive study *The Birth of the Messiah*). A helpful journal article in the area by an equally competent American New Testament scholar is that by J. A. Fitzmyer, "The Resurrection of Jesus Christ according to the New Testament," *The Month* (1987 November) 402–10. The scholars have surely helped us to make sense of these mysteries of Jesus' life.

It is interesting to note that all this scholarly study of New Testament theologians at work making sense of Jesus has for the last thirty years had the blessing of authoritative magisterial bodies in the Catholic community. We quoted from the Pontifical Biblical Commission's 1964 Instruction on the historical value of the Gospels, *Sancta Mater Ecclesia*, which the following year was condensed into a chapter on the New Testament in Vatican II's Constitution *Dei Verbum* on divine revelation and the Bible.

EXERCISES IN THEOLOGY

1. Are you in the habit of regarding the New Testament as a theology book, a miscellany of somewhat different theologies of Jesus; that is, different Christologies? Choose a passage in two or three New Testament books outside the Gospels that illustrate such different presentations of Jesus.
2. There are some passages in the *Acts of the Apostles* that resemble in miniature the overall structure of the Gospels (preparation for ministry, Jesus' ministry, Paschal Mystery): 1.21–22; 2.22–24; 10.36–41. Is there some common theological emphasis emerging from these "mini-Gospels," some similar interpretation of Jesus? Does it correspond with the Gospels in this respect?
3. Paul tells us nothing of the life of Jesus prior to the Supper. What does this say of Paul's Christology? Is it yours? Is it the Gospels'?

5

The theologian as martyr, bishop, catechist

Theology may be defined as making sense of faith, bringing our brains to bear on what we believe. Theologians like Paul and the evangelists tried to clarify and express their faith in Jesus by invoking patterns and paradigms with which they and their listeners/readers were familiar with from their scriptures, such as Son of Man, Anointed Ruler, Suffering Servant. For us as theologians the challenge is manifold: to recognize these underlying theological matrices stemming from earlier theology, and to appreciate the New Testament authors' own theologizing about Jesus. The volume of material in print on biblical theology in general and Old and New Testament theologies in particular indicates that the challenge is substantial.

For us, as we have noted, the challenge is also one of context. As the biblical composers theologized within their own contexts, we do so within ours. Bridging the two is required of us; and in the section "Some further reading" at the close of previous chapters we have suggested avenues to follow to achieve this. One of the factors of context in which we theologize is *time*: we are living in a world far removed from Conquest and Exile and Jesus' Paschal Mystery. We lack the immediacy to those events of the biblical authors, and are far removed even from them, so that their attempts to make sense of Jesus are also distant and possibly strange to us. Again biblical criticism can help us by recreating their world—literary, historical, geographical, social, religious, theological.

How did the generations of Christians closer to the biblical period respond to the traditions about God's action in Jesus? They had the great advantage of proximity—and not just temporal proximity but cultural as well. For them in those first centuries of the Christian era—as much a pagan society as Christian, of course—there was a sense of urgency of response to the Jesus event and a cultural affinity which we lack. They could resonate with the words of Paul and the evangelists in a ready way now lost to us, who have to struggle to recreate it.

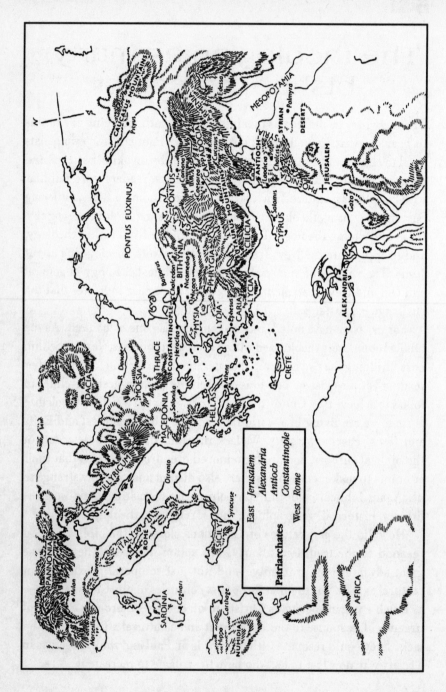

CAUCASUS MOUNTAINS
Pityus
MESOPOTAMIA
SYRIAN
DESERT
Palmyra
ARMENIA
PONTUS
ANTIOCH
Laodicea
Caesarea
CAPPADOCIA
TAURUS MOUNTAINS
CILICIA
Taurus
JERUSALEM
PHOENICIA
Gaza
PONTUS EUXINUS
Bosporus
CONSTANTINOPLE
Chalcedon
Nicomedia
Nicaea
BITHYNIA
GALATIA
CYPRUS
Salamis
Heraclea
Ephesus
CARIA
PHRYGIA
MYSIA
LYDIA
LYCIA
ALEXANDRIA
THRACE
R. Danube
DACIA
MOESIA
Salonika
MACEDONIA
HELLAS
Athens
CRETE
ILLYRICUM
Oronto
Ravenna
Syracuse
PANNONIA
Milan
ITALY
ROME
SICILY
SARDINIA
Cagliari
Marseilles
Hippo
Carthage
NUMIDIA
AFRICA

East   *Jerusalem*
        Alexandria
        Antioch
        Constantinople
West   *Rome*

Patriarchates

The World of the Fathers

FATHERS—AND MOTHERS—OF THE CHURCH

And this is the value to us of the early postbiblical theologians—pastors, catechists, preachers, writers, even martyrs who died to attest to their beliefs. They represent the first generations of believers, seeking understanding for their faith before even Augustine and Anselm. They are men and women, though owing to the culture of the time with its attitude to women's education and place in society the theology of men is much better documented. They live in both Western and Eastern divisions of the Roman Empire, governed from Rome and then also from Constantinople, and they share in the cultural differences of these two parts of the *oikoumene*, the inhabited world (Greek *oikos*, "house") as they knew it. As the Greek world is more speculative and the Roman more interested in discipline, so their theology—about Jesus and the Christian life—has a different character.

Until the Edict of (religious) Toleration in 313 under Constantine and Licinius and the former's eventual adoption of Christianity, this religion and its theology were under siege. Christianity was a minority religion, competing with Judaism and a range of other groups for survival and recognition, while also struggling to keep its own beliefs clear and uncontaminated. The large collection of gnostic scriptures discovered this century, including that "Fifth Gospel" and other Gospels lacking what was "of first importance" to Paul and the evangelists, indicate how difficult it was to establish "orthodoxy" in the generations immediately following Jesus. Where lay the Church, the community of his followers? What authority did it enjoy to prescribe belief, ritual and behavior for its members? Which writings, scriptures, were canonical or normative for the community?

For the earliest community "the scriptures" were, of course, those of Judaism, with which Jesus and his followers were well familiar and on which they were nourished. "Search the Scriptures," Jesus tells his Jewish adversaries when they contest his credentials (*Jn* 5.39), by which he meant *all* the Scriptures, not just the limited canon that the rabbis a century or so after his death drew up on ideological grounds. And an appeal to this tradition became normative for the early Church as further writings were added to "the Christian Scriptures" (a phrase that includes the Old Testament), such as Paul's letters to his communities or churches.

LIVING WORD OR DEAD TEXT?

But there were reservations about the utility of these new writings. The author of *2 Peter* (a late work, possibly second century) warns his own readers that in Paul's letters "there are some things hard to understand, which the ignorant and unstable twist to their own destruction, as they do the other scriptures" (3.16). In this we detect the early theologians inheriting the reluctance that rabbinic commentators on the Torah evinced, slow to commit their commentary to writing lest it be "twisted." Paul had no choice, of course, in writing to his missionary churches if he could not be there in person But there was a choice with the words of Jesus. Living Word or dead text? We are inclined to think that an inadequate *technology* was responsible for the late appearance of Jesus' life and words in textual form; but it was quite likely a *theological* difficulty that faced the early community: should they commit that Word to writing and thus lose control of it?

For a sense of the scruples of these early theologians we are indebted to the community's first great historian, Eusebius of Caesarea, after Constantine's time. He meticulously records the various attitudes to Gospel composition, which we should appreciate, if only because modern hermeneutical scholars like Hans-Georg Gadamer and Paul Ricoeur are coming round to the same sense of what it means to put word to text. Eusebius in his great *Church History* is professional enough to pass on to us six different accounts of the way the Gospels came to be put to writing, and many of them evince that reluctance to depart from a living Word. Papias, bishop of Hierapolis in Asia Minor around 130, gave his opinion:

> *If ever anyone came who had carefully followed the presbyters, I enquired as to the words of the presbyters, what Andrew or what Peter said, or what Philip or what Thomas or James or what John or Matthew or any other of the disciples of the Lord, and what Aristion and the presbyter John, the Lord's disciples, were saying. For I did not suppose that information from books helped me so much as that from a living and abiding voice* (emphasis added).

Justin, too, the convert from paganism who tells us about early Christian liturgies and who is martyred around 165, speaks of the biblical composers' work as oral rather than written. "We believe in the voice of God uttered through the apostles of Christ and announced to us through the prophets," he tells the Jew Trypho in his *Dialogue* with him.

But necessity and the pragmatic needs of missioners and apologists defending the faith overcame these theological scruples. As the community spread out to Africa and (modern) Europe, an apologist like Tertullian in Carthage around 200 could rejoice in Christianity's literary resources that enabled him to defend the faith against all comers:

> *The miracles (of the prophets) and the words they uttered in order to lead people to faith in the divinity are now kept in the treasury of literature, where they are available to us even now.*

Besides, there were other groups claiming the allegiance of Christians on the basis of false writings. The battle was on to determine the true canon, or normative collection, of the community's scriptures. Irenaeus, bishop of Lyons and Tertullian's contemporary, was (until the recent discovery of texts at Nag Hammadi in Egypt) our principal source of knowledge about the gnostic sects. He is insistent that there could be no such thing as a "Fifth Gospel."

> *It is impossible that the Gospels should be in number more or fewer than these. For since there are four regions of the world, and four principal winds, and since the Church is a seed planted in the whole earth, and the Gospel is the pillar and ground of the Church and the breath of life, it is natural that it should have four pillars, breathing incorruption from all quarters and kindling people into life.*

Theological argument yesterday and today, be it noted, especially in the heat of controversy, can often invoke more rationalizing than revealed truth! Still, in this early patristic period (see table), under the threat of persecution, there is not the latitude for theologians to reflect in full serenity.

Irenaeus is concerned about the integrity of the scriptural canon because of concern for the integrity of the community: error in the former could undermine the latter. (In fact, in his fierce opposition to gnostic error he includes and excludes from his canon what the community will finally rule on somewhat differently.) In this early period particularly, there is predictable theological effort put into supporting and delineating, if not precisely defining, the Christian Church, often against attack from sectarian Jewish and pagan groups. Apologists like Justin and Tertullian had come from within their ranks. The faithful had to be warned against these other groups' deficiencies; the fine line of orthodoxy was not yet clear, and people might make a "choice"— *hairesis* in Greek—which might prove in fact to be "heresy." Irenaeus writes a long work, *Detection and Overthrow of the Pretended but False Gnosis*, generally called "Against Heresies," delivering such a warning and proposing the remedy:

> *We should therefore avoid their heretical doctrines, and take care not to suffer injury from them, but flee to the Church, and be brought up in her bosom, and be nourished with the Lord's Scripture.*

CHURCH, ONE AND MANY

Of course, a Church under siege, not yet enjoying the necessary liberty for theological exploration, can easily proceed to extreme positions. An ardent apologist like Tertullian, as with many a convert, can rush to condemn all those not reaching an unrealistically high standard of observance and spirituality; the Montanist sect in which Tertullian died held that view. Irenaeus, by contrast, lived up to his name of "peacemaker" as well as his zeal as apologist by mediating in a dispute that threatened to divide the community around 190 under Pope Victor on the question of different dates for the celebration of Easter. He advised the pope not to rupture Church unity (*pax*, "peace"—as in the liturgy's "kiss of peace") by "ex-communicating" the group merely on the grounds of a different ritual for breaking the Lenten fast:

> *Such a diversity of observances has not just arisen now, in our time, but dates from long ago, from our forebears . . . They all nevertheless keep the peace (*pax*), as do we, one with another;* the difference in the fast confirms the agreement in the faith.

It is, of course, a vital theological principle: unity does not require utter uniformity; diversity can reinforce basic unity.

In contrast to Tertullian's eventual rigidity about Church membership and standards, his fellow convert Justin was even able to surpass Irenaeus's pragmatic tolerance of differences in Church practice and seek a theological explanation of the full extent of the Christian community. He had sampled all varieties of philosophical thought: Stoic, Peripatetic, Pythagorean, Platonic. After his conversion he left his native Palestine, came to Rome, founded a school there, engaged the Cynic philosopher Crescens in debate and composed his *Dialogue* with Jews. He could recognize good, and therefore the presence of the Word (*Logos*), in all good people—Christian, Jew, pagan—which can be seen germinating in the likes of Socrates. He thus left us with a model for seeing, as Vatican II finally does, the universal extent of relationship to Christ on the theological grounds of the presence of the Logos as a seed (*sperma*) sown in all humanity:

> *I confess that I boast and with all my strength strive to be found a Christian, not because the teachings of Plato are different from those of Christ, but because they are not in all respects similar, as neither are those of the others, Stoics and poets and historians. For each one spoke well in proportion to the share he had of the divine* Logos spermatikos . . .
>
> *For all the writers were able to see realities darkly through the sowing of the implanted Logos that was in them . . .*
>
> *For whatever either philosophers or lawgivers uttered well, they did so according to their share in discovering and contemplating the Logos. But since they did not know everything of the Logos, who is Christ, they often contradicted themselves.*

PRINCIPAL PERIODS OF PATRISTIC WRITING

I THE FIRST THREE CENTURIES

A. PRIMITIVE COMPOSITIONS AND APOSTOLIC FATHERS

	Apostles Creed	
	Didache	
	Clement of Rome	
64 Roman persecutions	Ignatius of Antioch	
	Polycarp of Smyrna	
	Papias	
	The Shepherd of Hermas	

B. APOLOGISTS AND CONTROVERSIALISTS

	Justin Martyr
martyrdom of Justin	Tatian
c.103	Irenaeus of Lyons

C. EARLY THEOLOGIANS AND CATECHISTS

	East	West
Roman Empire	Clement of Alexandria	Tertullian
divided East-West	Origen	Cyprian
293	Dionysius of Alexandria	Lactantius
		Hippolytus

II THE GOLDEN AGE; FOURTH AND FIFTH CENTURIES

	East		West
Edict of Toleration 313			
Conversion of Const.	**Alexandrians**	**Antiochenes**	Hilary of Poitiers
Council of Nicea 325	Athanasius	Theodore	Ambrose
Barbarians in Europe	Cappodocians	John Chrysostom	Jerome
Council of Constant. 381	.Basil	Eusebius of Caesarea	Augustine
Council of Ephesus 431	.Gregory of Nyssa		Paulinus of Nola
Council of Chalcedon 451	.Gregory Nazianzen		Pope Leo the Great
Vandals in Africa 429	Cyril of Alexandria		

III CLOSE OF PATRISTIC AGE; LATE FIFTH TO EIGHT CENTURIES

	East	West
last Roman Emperor 476	Dionysius the Areopagite	Benedict
birth of Mohammed 570	John Climacus	Gregory the Great (+604)
Augustine sent to	John Damascene (+740)	Isidore of Seville (+636)
England 597	Bede the Venerable (+735)	

THE THEOLOGY OF THE MAJORITY

Justin was well ahead of his time in pushing out the boundaries of theological exploration in this direction while his fellow apologists were content with manning the barricades as theologians of a minority. With the Edict of Toleration and Constantine's subsequent patronage of the Christian Church, the theological climate underwent a complete transformation. Membership of the once-persecuted community became respectable—in fact, obligatory. The difficulty would now lie in distinguishing, not the Christian group from other rival groups, but Church from State as imperial patronage built up this little flock into a powerful institution and brought pressure to bear on everyone to profess adherence. Theologians of the period, especially bishops in the West who presided over their churches like Roman officials over their jurisdictions, could now be found speaking of Church and sacraments in institutional terms on the model of civic society. It came to be presumed, with the freedom of missionaries to travel to all parts of the *oikoumene*, that everyone had had a chance to respond to the invitation of the Gospel; to be heretic or schismatic or otherwise independent meant liability to civic penalties.

It is in this climate of an ascendancy theology that we read statements from the Fathers in the West about sin, salvation and Church membership that, unlike those of Justin, are forbiddingly pessimistic. Augustine, bishop of Hippo in north Africa in the early fifth century, himself affected negatively by manichean and neoplatonic ideas regarding humanity and the world, and concerned about Pelagian optimism regarding free will, was influenced also by his African predecessor Cyprian of Carthage. Cyprian it was who was responsible for the exclusive dictum about Church membership, "Outside the Church no salvation," on that understanding that all people of good will had had the opportunity to respond to the Gospel invitation. He wrote in a letter:

> They cannot live outside, since there is only one house of
> God, and there can be no salvation except in the Church.

Augustine was prepared to take a lenient view of people living before the time of Jesus, and in Sermon 341 he admitted to the Church "all good people . . . from Abel the just one until the end of time" (which

Vatican II will quote with approval). But he was not happy with that New Testament expression of God's universal salvific will, "God desires everyone to be saved and to come to the knowledge of the truth" (*1 Tim* 2.4). In his view, arising from his previous and still unquenched heterodox associations, God had established "an unshakeable number of the elect"; the great number heading for perdition, the *massa damnata* in his phrase, would balance the ledger.

> *Neither those who have never heard the Gospel nor those*
> *who by reason of their infancy were unable to believe . . .*
> *are separated from that mass which will certainly be*
> *damned.*

SCHOOLS AND STYLES OF THEOLOGY

The pessimistic emphasis on sin and perdition in Western patristic theology, dominated as it is by Augustine's massive output, contrasts with the optimism of the East. Where the West thinks of the Fall, the East concentrates on our healing. Cyril of Alexandria, Theodore of Mopsuestia and Theodoret of Cyr are much more confident about the freedom of our will than is Augustine in his local polemic with Pelagius. As well, where the West is concerned with disciplinary matters, such as the administration of the sacraments, Eastern theologians are given to speculation. Irenaeus and Justin, whom we quoted for their relative flexibility and adventurous theologizing in early Western theology, in fact hailed from the East before arriving in Lyons and Rome respectively. It is no accident that all the Church councils of the first millennium were held in the East, the center of intellectual life. And the pity is that Western churchmen had little contact with their Eastern counterparts; Augustine, for instance, who had little knowledge of Greek, was generally ignorant of the patristic riches in that language.

Not that the Eastern church—which for predictable reasons of race, geography, language, diet and culture generally would almost inevitably be sundered from the West one day—was without its divisions and polemics. It was dominated by two contrasting schools of theology arising from two great ancient centers of learning, *Alexandria* (in Egypt) and *Antioch* (in Syria)—each with a more celebrated intellectual history than Rome or Carthage. The former, a center of Jewish learning that had contributed even to the Old Testament, was speculative in its thinking by comparison with the more pedestrian and pragmatic Antioch, "where the disciples were first called Christians" (*Acts* 11.26). The Alexandrian school brought a more spiritual approach to the Scriptures and to Jesus than did the Antiochene school, which insisted on the literal (as distinct from allegorical) sense of Scripture and the humanity of Jesus. These differences in theological approach fostered intense rivalry and surfaced in debates surrounding the first Church councils, as we shall see in the following chapter.

As the bulk of Augustine's literary remains dominates patristic theology in the West, that honor of voluminous extant work goes in the East to his contemporary John Chrysostom ("golden-mouthed," an epithet bestowed on him after his death), preacher in Antioch and then patriarch of Constantinople. He too lacked knowledge of Hebrew (as did most of the Fathers, except a great scholar like the catechist Origen), and could be uncritical in his approach to the biblical text, though as a good Antiochene he commented on it word by word. What he could contribute as an oriental theologian was twofold: his sense of divine transcendence—"ineffable," beyond words, is a habitual term of his— and as his own trademark an emphasis on divine considerateness, *synkatabasis*. This was manifested preeminently in the Incarnation and derivatively in the language of the Scriptures, taking account of human limitations. Vatican II's statement on the Bible, taking a leaf out of Pope Pius XII's earlier encyclical *Divino Afflante Spiritu*, acknowledges Chrysostom's theology of the Word in referring to this passage of his homily 17 on *Genesis* 3.8:

> *To learn from the very words God's ineffable*
> *considerateness (synkatabasis), you need to listen to what*
> *was read aloud: "They heard the Lord's voice as he walked*
> *in the garden in the evening, and Adam and his wife hid*
> *from the face of the Lord among the trees in the garden."*
> *Do not rush on quickly over things said in Sacred*
> *Scripture, beloved, nor stop short at the words themselves;*
> *instead, let us consider that the ordinariness of the words*
> *is made necessary by our limitations, and everything is*
> *done in the way God wants it for sake of our salvation. I*
> *mean, if we wanted to be restricted to the way the words*

go, and take the sense in a way unbefitting to God, there
would be no avoiding all sorts of absurdities.

No fire and brimstone here (though homily 6 on *Genesis* is spent upbraiding his congregation for deserting him to spend a day at the races!). No preoccupation with sin and damnation, no concern for disciplinary matters, such as might emerge from a Western commentary. Nor is there the rapid flight from the biblical text into fanciful allegorical interpretations, such as an Alexandrian commentator might be tempted to. Instead, a close verbatim *commentary* (not as precise as modern *exegesis*), emphasizing correlatively the transcendence of the divine and the real needs of the human listeners. Like Augustine, Chrysostom was convinced that his congregation's faith stood to gain from his theological elaboration, as he often reminded them. More than Augustine, his commentary rested not on rhetorical skills but on a firm grasp of the incarnation of the Word in the real world—inculturation, we call it today.

SOME FURTHER READING

Partly because of changing fashions, partly because of a decline in the knowledge of the classical languages, study of the Fathers of the Church lost a place in the curriculum of theological colleges for a period. This was not true of an earlier age, when John Henry Newman could claim of them (perhaps excessively: it is not the approach adopted above):

I follow the Fathers, not as thinking that on such a subject
(as the one under consideration) they have the weight they
possess in the instance of doctrines or ordinances. When
they speak of doctrines, they speak of them as being
universally held. They are witnesses to the fact of these
doctrines having been received, not here or there, but
everywhere. We receive these doctrines which they thus
teach, not merely because they teach them, but because
they bear witness that all Christians everywhere then held
them.

Newman's was the age when several major English translations of the Fathers were undertaken. Fortunately, this initiative has been continued in our day with two new series of translations, making the Fathers accessible: *The Fathers of the Church* series (Catholic University of America Press) and *Ancient Christian Writers* (Paulist Press). Chrysostom's *Homilies on Genesis* may be found in the former series (three volumes, my translation and commentary). So there is no excuse for unfamiliarity with these great theologians of yesterday. For further detail on the Fathers' attitude to Scripture, see my article "The Fathers on the Bible," *Pacifica* 7 (1994) 255–72, or Charles Kannengiesser, "The Bible as read in the early Church: patristic exegesis and its presuppositions," *Concilium* 1991/1 (*The Bible and its Readers*)29–36.

If you are not prepared to embark on reading the hundreds of volumes of the Fathers, you may settle for a potted version of what they have to say on a whole range of topics. The *Message of the Fathers of the Church* series (Michael Glazier) runs to at least 22 volumes, summarizing their teaching on topics like Church, Biblical Interpretation, Eucharist, Ministry, Women in the Early Church. New City, London, has begun a series on *The Spirituality of the Fathers*, author by author. As to the writings of or about the Mothers of the Church, which we admitted were not so well preserved, Joanne Turpin has compiled *Women in Church History. 20 Stories for 20 Centuries* (Cincinnatti: St Anthony Messenger Press, 1990). The social stereotype that contributed to the paucity of women's literary remains did not die with the patristic age; as late as 1837 the English poet Robert Southey rejected poems sent by a young woman (by name Charlotte Bronte) with this curt dismissal:

> *Literature cannot be the business of a woman's life, and it ought not to be. The more she is engaged in her proper duties, the less leisure she will have for it, even as an accomplishment.*

Southey, proved wrong in this case, need only have looked at the fourth-century life of Gregory of Nyssa's sister Macrina, who is credited with completing the education of their more famous brother Basil:

> *He was puffed up beyond measure with the pride of oratory and looked down on all the local dignitaries, excelling in his own estimation all the leading men. Nevertheless Macrina took him in hand, and with such speed did she draw him also toward the mark of philosophy that he forsook the glories of this world.*

The Catholic community has recently advocated renewed study of these great theologians in an *Instruction on the Study of the Fathers of the Church in the Formation of Priests* (Rome: Vatican Press, 1989)—though their value, of course, is for theologians clerical and nonclerical. A simple introduction to this study, patrology, is Boniface Ramsay's *Beginning to Read the Fathers* (London: DLT, 1980). The classic introduction in four volumes is Johannes Quasten's *Patrology* (Newman and Christian Classics), with assistance from Angelo Di Berardino—a real "Christian Classic." For a conspectus of the Fathers' teaching on major theological areas, see J. N. D. Kelly, *Early Christian Doctrines* (5th ed., San Francisco: Harper and Row, 1978). And in this electronic age the (Latin) Fathers are going on to CD-ROM, courtesy of Brepols, Belgium—a decisive development for the aid of researchers.

EXERCISES IN THEOLOGY

1. Go to the theological library you customarily visit, and look at the patristic section. In particular, seek out the series of translations of the Fathers. By preference, find Eusebius's *Ecclesiastical History* and in Book 3 see if you can locate the several accounts of the writing of the Gospels. If not Eusebius, find another of the Fathers' works and read enough to get its flavor.

2. The patristic age suggests that a persecuted Church theologizes differently from a community enjoying peace and prosperity. Can we see parallels of both styles of theology in today's world?

3. The Eastern Church is hugely represented in patristic theology, with all its strengths and some weaknesses, and yet we have lost touch with it. Take a modern theological work and examine it for its acquaintance with that half of the Church (or with the Fathers generally).

Forging a language for theology

What theology brings to faith is reflection, pondering, the search for sense and meaning, even precise statement and perhaps eventually system. In Chapter 1 we caviled at Karl Rahner's presumption that all theology involves "conscious and methodical explanation and explication" of faith. That is certainly not true of all our theologizing, though we are grateful for some formulations of belief (if not all). The degree of method and system can vary from age to age. The patristic period demonstrates both the theology of a minority under pressure and a patronized majority's theologizing in peace and prosperity.

AREAS OF THEOLOGY

It is interesting and instructive to compare the theological concerns and preoccupations and processes of the two groups, persecuted and patronized. The former we saw struggling to maintain the identity of the Christian Church and its reasonable claim to existence in a world in which philosophies and religious sects abounded. The Scriptures, including both Old and New Testaments, were appealed to by the apologists as source material in this debate. Some Fathers could admit the acceptability of (some) other scriptures and other religious groups alongside Christianity. In these debates the Christian God and the centrality of Jesus' life and death figured constantly. Disciplinary and liturgical questions arose, especially in the West, in connection with the administration of the Church's rites, the sacraments.

With the coming of religious toleration, this *ad hoc* approach to theologizing and the accent on identity recede, and depth is given to study of central doctrines, especially the Trinity and Christology. Theologians are free to delve into further areas, like the Fall, sin, salvation/redemption, grace, and different approaches to ecclesiology and the sacraments. In place of an external persecution, the stimulus to public theology now becomes self-inflicted, as it were. Intense rivalries between theological schools, and the appearance of splinter groups—

heresies, if you like—means the line of orthodoxy is drawn more securely. At least in the East theological debate becomes "flavor of the month" for every Tom, Dick and Harry. As Gregory of Nyssa describes of the late fourth century, bakers, money-changers, bath attendants, all have their view on the most moot doctrinal distinction.

It becomes possible in this climate of freedom and introspection to draw up a theological manifesto of Christian faith, to which all hopefully might subscribe and which might put paid to all acrimony and division. Most religions attempt to offer as much to their adherents, and profession of it can be a requirement of adherence. Over and over again there appears, for instance, in the Jewish Scriptures a recital of faith, not casual but carefully theologized, which expresses what that people thought of their God, his relationship with them and therefore their identity. The great literary-theological critic Gerhard Von Rad believed he had found such statements in the work of the Deuteronomist and in prophetic literature. He called them "cultic credos" because they occur in (para)liturgical situations. The worshipper is required to express belief while performing a ritual—such as presentation of first fruits of the harvest:

> When the priest takes the basket from your hand and sets it down before the altar of the Lord your God, you shall make this response before the Lord your God:
> "A wandering Aramean [Jacob] was my ancestor; he went down into Egypt and lived there as an alien, few in number, and there he became a great nation, mighty and populous.
> When the Egyptians treated us harshly and afflicted us, by imposing hard labor on us, we cried to the Lord, the God of our ancestors; the Lord heard our voice and saw our affliction, our toil, and our oppression.
> The Lord brought us out of Egypt with a might hand and an outstretched arm, with a terrifying display of power, and with signs and wonders;
> and he brought us into this place and gave us this land, a land flowing with milk and honey.
> So now I bring the first fruit . . ." (Dt 26.5–10).

An almost identical creed occurs at 6.20–25, where the situation is a Passover meal or some other Jewish ritual at which a child might be likely to raise questions, for which a formula is ready. Von Rad calls them also "a credal salvation-history" because, in the mind of the Deuteronomist at least, what is vital to Jewish faith is what God has done for the people—a narrative including certain basic articles or beliefs:

- God chose them (a choice demonstrated in the patriarchs—often Abraham, here Jacob);
- God delivered them from slavery in the marvels of the Exodus;
- God led them into the Land.

A NARRATIVE CREED

It is interesting to see what is included in this recital of (theologized) faith. It is a narrative of events, God's doings, not a list of divine attributes, though elsewhere the Old Testament will list these (cf *Pss* 117; 139). (It is also interesting to see what is excluded, at least from this Deuteronomic creed: the Decalogue, for instance.) The people believe they can recognize themselves in this account of divine beneficence (toward them only). The *language* of faith and theology here is not that of piety, nor philosophy, but narrative (and in *Dt*'s characteristically repetitive style, though this is accidental). So in this creed about Israel's God the accent falls on function, not on essence—on *God Who Acts*, in the title of a book by a disciple of Von Rad, G. Ernest Wright.

We have seen Paul summarizing the faith of the Christian community in similar narrative terms: Jesus died, Jesus rose (*1 Cor* 15). The Gospels and mini-Gospels, too, take narrative form in communicating what is basic about Jesus' life and death. They vary in length, but we saw the structure to have been theologized in three (or fourfold) form with the accent falling, as in Paul, on the Paschal Mystery. The community's theologians have concurred that the stress should fall on soteriology, on what God does (for us) in Jesus rather than who Jesus is, on function rather than on essence. Paul knows other professions of faith as well: "We proclaim Jesus Christ as Lord," he assures the Corinthians (*2 Cor*

53

4.5) in another well-rehearsed formula. And he tries to explain for them the relationship of Jesus with the Father and with all creation:

> For us there is one God, the Father, from whom are all
> things and for whom we exist,
> and one Lord, Jesus Christ, through whom are all things
> and through whom we exist (1 Cor 8.6).

In a world of diverse philosophies, however, not to mention varying shades of Christian belief, simple narrative statement might not suffice. Even in the New Testament there is admission of the difficulty for some in accepting the Incarnation. "Every spirit that confesses that Jesus Christ has come in the flesh is from God, and every spirit that does not confess Jesus is not from God," warns the author of *1 John* 4.2–3. Ignatius of Antioch, martyred in Rome before the New Testament was complete, likewise contests such docetic tendencies querying the reality of Jesus' humanity: "He did not suffer merely in appearance, as some of the unbelievers say . . . As for me, I know that even after his rising he was in the flesh." We have noted gnostic downplaying of Jesus' Paschal Mystery, vital to the Pauline creed. Believers in Jesus with a Jewish background, if not a prey to the dualistic attitudes to him stemming from these docetic and gnostic groups, had their own problems about Trinitarian and Christological belief, arising from strong Jewish monotheism. A great historian of the early community, Alois Grillmeier, remarks of them:

> An absolutely closed Judaistic monotheism necessarily
> brings adoptionism in its train. We have reached the point
> where Church teaching had to develop Trinitarian and
> Christological dogma side by side if it was to maintain the
> divine Sonship of Christ in the true sense.

A LANGUAGE FOR THEOLOGY

So the theologians of the emancipated Christian community were faced with the task of forging a language to give adequate expression to faith; mere narrative would no longer suffice. The task was rendered more difficult, not just because of the current heterodox views, but owing to the intense rivalry of theological schools associated with Alexandria and Antioch, referred to in Chapter 5. The former, long a Jewish center of scholarship and thus perhaps inheriting the tendencies of which Grillmeier speaks, was also under the spell of Platonic philosophy. It thus tended to adopt an allegorical approach to Scripture, thanks to the influence of the great catechist Origen. Alexandrian theologians were thus impatient of the more down-to-earth Antiochene school, Aristotelian in philosophy, literal if not literalist in its approach to Scripture, and correspondingly insistent on the humanity of Jesus. Consensus between these rival schools in philosophy, terminology, approach to Scripture and theology was out of the question, and theological differences became politicized.

Ironically, it was the emperor Constantine—lately converted from paganism, if not yet baptized, and certainly not able to recognize theological niceties—who convoked the first of a series of councils of the Church from all parts of the "inhabited world," *oikoumene*, and thus known as "ecumenical." These councils met in the East, reflecting the center of intellectual activity in this age (as well as the relative insecurity in the troubled West), and were in the shadow of imperial Constantinople. The first, at Nicea in 325, addressed the subordinationist views about Jesus held by Arius, priest of Alexandria, but blamed by the Alexandrians on Antiochene literalist exegesis. Athanasius of Alexandria leads the charge, a creed is produced in which occurs a key term *homoousios*, "of the same substance," to assert the equality of Father and Son. All accept the Council's term and creed, but then proceed to interpret them differently according to their own philosophical systems and develop their own theological approaches to Jesus and Trinity. Another council convenes at Constantinople in 381, produces a more developed creed that we tend to call erroneously "Nicene," and hopes the problem is solved. Its central article reads:

> *We believe in one Lord, Jesus Christ, the only Son of God,*
> *eternally begotten of the Father,*
> *God from God, light from light,*
> *true God from true God,*
> *begotten, not made,*
> *of one being (*homoousios*) with the Father.*

> ## First Seven Ecumenical Councils
>
> 325 Nicea I
>
> 381 Constantinople I
>
> 431 Ephesus
>
> 451 Chalcedon
>
> 553 Constantinople II
>
> 680-81 Constantinople III
>
> 787 Nicea II

COUNCILS, CREEDS AND FORMULAS

An Introduction to theology like this is not the place to explore the Christological and Trinitarian teachings of the various councils and the significance of creeds and formulas produced by them, nor the teachings of the theologians declared to be in error. Systematic theology in its various branches deals with those. Here it is appropriate to discern the avenues being followed by the theologians of the time in dealing with the challenge that faith in Trinity and Jesus poses. Suffice it to add that, in the wake of the 381 council, efforts to explore further the implications of those creeds conducted at Antioch under the name of the priest Nestorius were violently resisted at Alexandria under Cyril, whose own argumentation sounds suspicious today. A council was convoked at Ephesus in 431, and at what historian J. N. D. Kelly calls "an astonishing medley of rival meetings," Cyril with an assembly of likeminded bishops (the Third Ecumenical Council!) condemned Nestorius.

Predictably, all theological problems did not then disappear, nor did the rivalries of schools. In fact, a further difficulty about Jesus' humanity and divinity arose shortly afterwards, partly due to misunderstanding of key terms in the debate, "nature" and "person," taken differently by the rival schools and their philosophies. The West intervened, uniquely, in the person of Pope Leo, and a council was held at Chalcedon with a formula produced which was intended to settle the matter once and for all. It reads:

Following the holy Fathers [of previous councils], we
unanimously teach that our Lord Jesus Christ is one and
the same Son,
the same perfect in divinity and the same perfect in humanity,
true God and true man, consisting of a rational soul and
a body,
consubstantial with the Father in divinity and
consubstantial with us in humanity, "like us in all things
except sin" [Heb 4.15],
born of the Father before all time as to his divinity, born
in recent times for us and for our salvation from the
Virgin Mary, Mother of God, as to his humanity.

We confess one and the same Christ, the Son, the Lord, the
Only-begotten,
in two natures unconfused, unchangeable, undivided and
inseparable.
The difference of natures (physis) will never be abolished
by their being united,
but rather the properties of each remain unimpaired,
both coming together in one person (prosopon) and one
substance (hypostasis),
not parted or divided among two persons (prosopa),
but in one and the same only-begotten Son, the divine
Word, the Lord Jesus Christ, as previously the prophets and
Jesus Christ himself taught us and the Creed of the Fathers
handed down to us.

This is the "last word" in "classical" Christology, in more ways than
one. Never again, not even at Vatican II, did the community attempt a
definition of the "hypostatic union" of the divine and the human in
Jesus. Not that all difficulties disappeared and rival schools fell silent.
Not that our own times have not engendered all kinds of Christological
problems. Rather, it comes down to the question: how successful were
the councils and the creeds and the formulas in forging a language for
theology? Let us evaluate their efforts.

EVALUATING THEOLOGICAL LANGUAGE

It needs to be remembered that conciliar statement was very much conditioned by the concepts and idioms of contemporary (Eastern) philosophy, or different philosophies—humanity, divinity, nature, person, hypostasis, substance (terms not always employed univocally). Even if this context is accepted, Christians today can be repelled by such terminology, and have difficulty relating to the Jesus of such statements, as to Byzantine art. They find it all very remote and thus tend to ask themselves:

• If language is about communication, and if theology is intended to bring clarity and understanding to faith, we have to wonder if, in departing from the directness and simplicity of Gospel narrative, these councils and creeds were more likely to bring to believers of their time (and ours) a clear picture of Jesus.

• Council discussions were often conducted in polemical terms and their creeds and formulas drafted after harsh controversy; so they hardly modeled the Jesus of the Beatitudes, however much they talked of his nature and person.

• So, Christologists complain that the councils' way of talking about Jesus is not "from below"—from a life led like ours, from consideration of the human condition which Jesus shares with us—but "from above," which means beginning with the fact of God's "coming down" to take a human nature, emphasizing therefore the preexistence of the Word.

• A corollary of this emphasis in conciliar, classical Christology is that it concentrates on the Incarnation—the moment of the "union of two natures in one person"—whereas the New Testament is unanimous in stressing the Paschal Mystery in Jesus' life and is prepared if necessary to omit the Incarnation and infancy (as we saw in Paul, the Gospels and mini-Gospels).

• Perhaps another way of saying this is that the council statements seem to present Jesus as a problem to be solved instead of as a savior come to redeem us. What Jesus does (for us) is, in the biblical view, at least as important as what he is.

• There is also the omission of the ministry of Jesus in the council statements, even though many Christians would find this period of Jesus' life the most rewarding for insights into this unique person—the miracles of Jesus, his parables, sermons and other sayings. Is theology supplying a corrective to piety and devotion here?

• Whatever happened to the mystery of Christ in council formulas? Concentration on the person of Jesus led the conciliar theologians to ignore the context in which Jesus occurs, the totality of the divine plan for all things.

• Finally, there is about the whole conciliar debate concerning Jesus the suspicion that we are witnessing only a war of words, which might have been solved had the opposing parties paused to listen to each other's use of words—sometimes the same words understood differently (*physis, hypostasis, prosopon, homoousios*). This is never true of the drama of Jesus' life portrayed in the New Testament; it was not for a word that he died, but for our salvation.

A much more positive and nuanced appreciation of the contribution of council theology is that of the late Karl Rahner in an article entitled "Chalcedon—end or beginning?":

> *Work by the theologians and teachers of the Church bearing on a reality and a truth revealed by God always ends in an exact formulation. This is natural and necessary. For only in this way is it possible to draw a line of demarcation, excluding heresy and misunderstanding of the divine truth, which can be observed in everyday religious practice. But if the formula is thus an end, the result and victory which bring about simplicity, clarity, the possibility of teaching and doctrinal certainty, then in this victory everything depends on the end also being seen as a beginning.*

SOME FURTHER READING

The conciliar period of the community's theologizing illustrates the articulation of community *faith* into clearly defined *beliefs*. This is a distinction Richard McBrien makes in speaking of "*doctrines* (beliefs elevated to the level of official approbation), *dogmas* (doctrines that carry the highest level of official approbation, the denial of which normally separates one from the community of faith)." In his helpful article "Faith, theology and belief" (in M. Warren, ed., *Source Book for Modern Catechetics*, Winona: St Mary's Press, 1982) he sees belief as a product of the process of theologizing about faith.

This period is well documented. The official collection of creeds and formulas and decrees, at least for the Catholic community, is one edited originally by Henry Denzinger (d.1888) and since by fellow Jesuits. It is now known as Denzinger-Schönmetzer (DS), *Enchiridion Symbolorum, Definitionum et Declarationum de rebus fidei et morum*. As statements are included in their original languages, a knowledge of Greek and Latin is required for optimum use. The new *Catechism* therefore, while citing DS, employs a modern translation, that by J. Neuner and J. Dupuis, *The Christian Faith in the Doctrinal Documents of the Catholic Church*, Cork: Mercier, 1983. A collection of documents of the conciliar period is J. Stevenson's *Creeds, Councils and Controversies*, London: SPCK, 1981.

The classic historian of these early centuries of theology is Alois Grillmeier in his volumes of *Christ in Christian Tradition*, which are gradually being translated into English. Grillmeier is so infatuated with his subject that he is inclined to take unduly rosy views of the efficacy of the councils' decisions, as in these words on the Chalcedon formula (which we might wonder if the bishops themselves understood):

> *The simple, original proclamation of Christ, the revealer and bringer of salvation, the proclamation of Christ the Son of God can be heard in undiminished strength through all the* philosophoumena *of the Fathers.*

R. H. Fuller is more nuanced in his evaluation of conciliar statement:

> *The church has to proclaim the Gospel into the contemporary situation. And that is precisely what the Nicene [sic] Creed and the Chalcedonian formula were trying to do . . . This is the task of the proclaiming church, and, in a specialized sense, of systematic theology in each succeeding age. It cannot simply go on repeating either the* . *New Testament kerygma (which is couched in terms of obsolete mythologies) or the orthodox formulae (which are couched in terms of an obsolete metaphysic).*

Early Christian Creeds, J. N. D. Kelly's companion volume to his *Early Christian Doctrines*, is another helpful commentary of his.

I have suggested, along with Pauline thought, that a key concept for theology is that of the mystery of Christ, the big picture in which the coming of Jesus is to be situated as a critical (perhaps focal) point of the whole divine plan. The councils in the heat of controversy tended, myopically, to home in on Jesus as a problem to be solved, thus forfeiting the light shed on him (as all contexts do) by consideration of the larger pattern, or "mystery." For a developed exploration of this thought, see my *Jesus and the Mystery of Christ. An Extended Christology*, Melbourne: CollinsDove, 1993.

The question of theology's proper mode of expression continues to be debated and modeled variously in theological writing. Marie-Dominique Chenu has this to say:

> *If the Christian plan or "economy" is accomplished through the Word of God in a revelation adapted to human speech and human truth, then it is both natural and necessary that the actual words should take priority in the conditions of worldly intercourse. God remains a stranger to the people whose language the missionary speaks no better than a passing traveler, and his truth finds no place in a school where grammar and exegesis are neglected. From this simple origin arises the Church's attachment to dogmatic formulas. Words, in which the faith takes flesh, are the raw material not only of the catechist but also of the professional theologian. One might even say that the theologian is primarily a philologist from the moment he seeks to understand and elaborate his belief.*

Chenu, perhaps unaware that he is mouthing the insights also of John Chrysostom and the doctrine of "considerateness" we noted in the preceding chapter, has the medieval scene in mind; but he is touching on a modern problem in theology as well. Vatican II in its statements on priestly formation (#16) and divine revelation (#24) recommends a change in theological language by making Scripture "the soul of theology." Not all scholars have so far responded, preferring philosophical categories for the conduct of theological investigation.

EXERCISES IN THEOLOGY

1. Get hold of the text of both the Apostles Creed (perhaps 2nd century) and the Niceno-Constantinople Creed, and compare them on grounds of theological precision and pastoral effectiveness. Which do you think would function better in the eucharistic celebration? Is the Sunday Eucharist the most appropriate locus for recitation of the community's creed? Is there a better?

2. Would you agree with the view of John Paul II in his 1994 book *Crossing the Threshold of Hope*, "The words of the Nicene Creed are nothing other than the reflection of Paul's doctrine" (47)?

3. Read again the Chalcedonian formula given above. For whom was it intended, would you think? To what extent does it incorporate the language that theology wants to employ? Compare it with statements of Vatican II on Jesus (e.g., in *Gaudium et Spes*).

4. We saw Karl Rahner claiming a victory for early council creeds and formulas, winning for us simplicity and clarity and the possibility of teaching, along with doctrinal certainty. Thus misunderstanding is avoided, he maintains. Why do you think Vatican II did not adopt that style of expression? Have you read works that seem to aspire to Rahner's model for theological idiom?

7

Bringing system to theology

Theology should help to meet the human being's innate need to have things make sense. If God's in his heaven, all should be right with the world. There's got to be a pattern, a plan—or what's faith for? In one of his novels, *The Gift of Asher Lev*, Chaim Potok has Asher and his wife Devorah discussing her terrible wartime experience of being concealed in a Paris apartment to avoid capture by the Gestapo. The film *Au Revoir Les Enfants*, about Jewish children killed in the Holocaust, has awoken fearful memories for her.

> *I held her. She was trembling.*
> *"Isn't it strange that I can't remember what we ate? Two years of eating in that sealed apartment, and I can't remember a single meal. Asher, I am not sorry we saw the movie. It's a fine movie. Even though sometimes, sitting in a dark theater, I suddenly remember the dark apartment. If it's all God's will, my husband, there must be a plan. Don't you think there must be a plan?"*
> *"Who knows? Maybe there's a plan."*

THE SEARCH FOR MEANING

Qoheleth in Old Testament times, despite the bewildering national calamities that perhaps explain his radical skepticism, was sure there is a plan. "For everything there is a season, and a time for every matter under heaven," he concludes, rather fatalistically (*Eccl* 3.1). Paul more positively could speak of "the mystery of Christ," gathering up all things, "things in heaven and things on earth" (*Eph* 1.10)—even if this plan meant the astonishing development that the Gentiles had become fellow heirs, members of the same body, and sharers in Christ Jesus through the Gospel (3.6). Not every deliberate plan of God is in keeping with the expectations of theologians, Paul has to admit:

> *O the depths of the riches and wisdom and knowledge of God! How unsearchable are his judgments and how inscrutable his ways* (Rom 11.33).

Just as the modern muse wonders, "What's it all about, Alfie?", so theologians from the beginning have not been content with occasional insights into those divine judgments and ways. Biblical narrative and prophecy and Wisdom and apocalyptic and lyric are notoriously piecemeal and at times contradictory. The Bible, with all its styles and books and authors and dates of composition, is calling out for order, synthesis. It is no theological textbook, though it has long been mined for gems to titivate such books (not quite what Vatican II had in mind when seeing its role as "the soul of theology").

THE SYSTEM OF THE RABBIS

At least from the time of return from Exile, Jewish scholars in academies and rabbis in synagogues responded to this need to impose order on biblical disorder. The Talmud is a vast body of theological scholarship which builds up in varied mosaic style a legal and narrative pattern arising out of generations of scholarly comment on scriptural texts. In the Mishnah, scholars accumulated layer upon layer of oral comment on the written text, an oral Torah commenting on the written Torah. It was finally codified in systematic form two centuries after rabbi Jesus and complemented by Gemara and Tosefta ("additions") in the academies of Palestine and Babylon for four further centuries. The

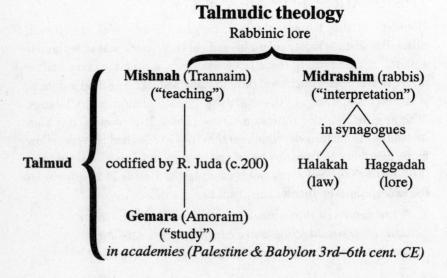

Talmudic theology
Rabbinic lore

Mishnah (Trannaim)   **Midrashim** (rabbis)
("teaching")   ("interpretation")

in synagogues

Talmud   codified by R. Juda (c.200)   Halakah   Haggadah
                                           (law)   (lore)

Gemara (Amoraim)
("study")
in academies (Palestine & Babylon 3rd–6th cent. CE)

Mishnah (from *shanah*, "repeat") is systematically arranged in six "orders" consisting of 63 tractates, each divided into chapters (523 in all), which are subdivided into paragraphs.

In the less academic synagogues from the time of the scribe Ezra, who "had set his heart to study (*darash*) the Law of the Lord" (*Ezra 7.10*), a particular style of commentary on the biblical text also emerged, *midrash*, combining law (*halakah*) and lore (*haggadah*), legal and narrative material. "The sacred words became an inexhaustible mine," says A. Cohen, "which, when quarried, produced rich treasures of religious and ethical teaching." For instance, in a midrash on *Exodus 20.21* ("I [Heb. *anokhi*] am the Lord your God") we read:

> *Rabbi Aha said: For twenty-six generations the Hebrew letter* alef *complained bitterly to the Almighty: I am the first letter [of the alphabet], and yet Thou didst not create the world with me but only with [the second letter]* beth, *namely,* b'reshith *["In the beginning God created:" Gn 1.1]. But the Almighty appeased her: By your life! I will recompense you: My world and its fulness were created only for the sake of the Torah—as it says: The Lord established the world for the sake of Wisdom [Prv 3.19]. The Torah was created 2000 years before the world, and when I come to give it to Israel I will commence with you:* anokhi, *I, am the Lord your God.*

Rabbinic learning, or Talmudic theology, thus consists of Mishnah, "teaching," and midrashim, "interpretation"—a massive and fascinating theological system.

We may wonder how systematic in fact is the rabbis' commentary on TaNaK, and indeed whether biblical statement is susceptible of systematization at all. The Christian Fathers and medievals thought it was; they could find in their Scriptures as much as the rabbis, if put to it. So the Word of God for Chrysostom is a complete reference book, with moral and hagiographic value as well:

> *If you want to talk about a king, there is a king in these stories; if it's about soldiers, or family matters, or public affairs, you will see a great abundance of these examples in the Scriptures. Examples of this kind are of great*

*benefit. It would in fact be impossible—impossible, I say—
for a soul nourished on these stories to be overcome by
passion.*

Closer to medieval times Cassiodorus closes his commentary on the *Psalms* with similar conviction that their content is truly encyclopedic:

*See, we have shown that the series of Psalms is filled with
grammar and etymologies, with schemata, with the art of
rhetoric, with topica, with the art of dialectics, with music,
with geometry, with astronomy, and with the expressions
peculiar to the divine law.*

His final word on the subject is: "What information can you fail to find in that heavenly treasury of the divine Scriptures?"

A BIBLICAL ENCYCLOPEDIA

Those words proved a challenge to patristic and medieval students of the Bible. Scriptural texts could not only be shown to refer to such a vast range of topics, but any one could be interpreted in a multiplicity of ways. There is the literal or historical sense, but also a number of spiritual senses variously listed—"allegorical" and "anagogical," in the terminology of Augustine's contemporary, John Cassian (which Gregory the Great at the close of the patristic period will combine under a "typical" sense), and a "tropological" sense (which for Gregory is "moral"). A medieval tag ran as follows:

*Lettera gesta docet, quid credas allegoria,
moralis quid agas, quo tendas anagogia.*

*The literal sense tells you what happened, the allegorical
what to believe,
the moral what to do, the anagogical whither to direct
your thoughts.*

Take as an example their interpretation of references in the biblical text to Jerusalem. Literally, it is a city of the Jews; allegorically, the Church of Christ; anagogically, that heavenly city to which we must tend; and tropologically or morally, our soul on which the Lord draws blessings or admonitions.

**classic medieval listing of
four senses of Scripture**

[1 literal/historical, 3 spiritual]

Example: JERUSALEM

1. **literal/historical**
   a city of the Jews

2. **allegorical**
   the Church of Christ

   } **typical**

3. **anagogical**
   the heavenly city beckoning us

4. **tropological**   **moral**
   our soul, which God blesses and chides

Understandably, the imaginative hermeneutical efforts of these biblical commentators, though obeying certain conventions, would not satisfy all who wanted to bring the cold light of reason to faith. And in the age that produced the wonderfully designed cathedrals of Europe, emerging from the dark ages that threatened now to beset the East, order and synthesis and system was wanted in the theological schools that were being founded in Salamanca, Bologna, Naples, Paris and Oxford. The Scriptures, interpreted not spiritually but literally ("All other senses of Sacred Scripture are based on the literal," was Aquinas's dictum), would remain the basic text. But in place of hermeneutical extravagance there came to hand the pragmatic philosophy of Aristotle and Avicenna. What Augustine never attempted and even Anselm six centuries later, despite his rationalism, could not achieve, Bonaventure and Aquinas and John Duns Scotus found possible. Theology was to prove itself as a science.

A MEDIEVAL SYSTEM

These men were all members of religious orders, but they brought theology out of the monasteries into the fledgling universities and applied a relatively rigorous and critical approach to their reading of statements of faith, like the Bible. After the reading (*lectio*) to the class came a questioning (*quaestio*) addressed to the text on some textual or doctrinal matter within it. We might now regard some of these as "Dorothy Dix" type questions, artificially proposed, but they served as scholastic devices to engage student and text and teacher—a "scholastic" model as distinct from devotional or homiletic approaches.

If the method involved rigor, the overall design required both comprehensiveness (to be a *summa*, as the name suggests) as well as theological insight and integrity. It was the merit of Thomas Aquinas, commenting on the Gospels to his students in the Schools of Naples, that he designed a three-stage course as theologically satisfying as those great gothic cathedrals lifting their spires to heaven. In Part I he presents God as the author of all things; he studies human behavior in Part II, devoted to the way back to God; Part III, the specifically Christian way back, encompasses Christ and the sacraments. Beyond this structural merit, Aquinas to some extent drew on the optimism of Eastern theology in defiance of Augustine's negative view of human nature. Chenu, a noted commentator on Thomism, remarks:

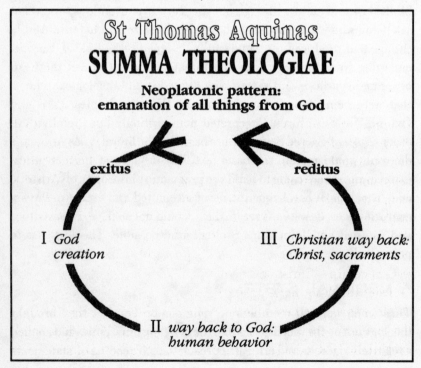

68

"It is a fact that every time this oriental theology filters westward it is at once received with reserve, sometimes with hostility. Its cosmic and Christological optimism is rather shocking to the mind of the west, dominated as it is by the Augustinian view of the universe and of sinful humanity." Aquinas to some extent demurred.

In fact, Aquinas's system and approach was itself found shocking. When professing in the University of Paris, he was opposed by the majority of theologians. He was condemned for his use of Aristotle on the grounds that his methods were too rationalistic and his attitude too naturalistic—the very things that recommended him to his contemporaries in humanities and liberal arts and that recommend him to us. From a theological point of view, on the other hand, while noting his rehabilitation by the establishment to the point where canon law made mandatory the formation of clergy "according to the method, the doctrine and the principles of the Angelic Doctor," some aspects of the *Summa* give us pause today.

A SYSTEM'S ADEQUACY

We have noted a shift in the theological center of gravity from Exodus and Paschal Mystery in the Scriptures to the Incarnation in conciliar creeds as the moment of the hypostatic union. We saw, too, a shift in accent from the soteriological—what God does for us—to the ontological, the essential—who Jesus is. A theologian like the medieval systematizers had to make a critical structural decision as to overall design. As emerges from our table, Aquinas chose neither Incarnation nor Paschal Mystery as the center of gravity. He opted instead for the neoplatonic pattern of *exitus* and *reditus*—the emanation of all things from God and their return to him. It is not a biblical pattern, though it has biblical similarities. It enables Aquinas to combine both *dogmatic* theology, truths about God and human beings and all creation (I), with *moral* theology, our way back to God (II), and the specifically Christian ways of return—Christ, the sacraments (III).

Paul would not be in agreement; but it was an age when biblical theology as such was not to the fore to the same extent as the mining of the Scriptures for isolated texts, even if Aquinas avoided a spiritual exegesis of these. Paul, with his insistence on what is "of first importance"—namely, "Jesus died, Jesus rose"—would have been aghast that the Paschal Mystery is left to Part III of the *Summa* and receives there less attention than the fourteen questions devoted to angels—in Part I! Aquinas sounds utterly logical—if logic is to be the prime criterion in theology—in opening Part III thus:

> *Our savior, the Lord Jesus Christ, in order to save his people from their sins, as the angel testifies (Mt 1.21), showed to us in his very person the way of truth, whereby by rising again we may reach the beatitude of immortal life. Hence it is necessary for the completion of the work of theology that we should now consider, after our study of the ultimate end of human life and of the virtues and vices, the savior of all people and the benefits bestowed by him on the human race.*
>
> *In this connection there is need to consider firstly the savior himself; secondly his sacraments, which are the means by which we attain salvation; thirdly the goal of immortal life, which we reach by rising through him.*
>
> *On the first of these points is a twofold consideration: the first deals with the very mystery of the Incarnation, by which God became man for our salvation; the second deals with the things that were done and suffered by our savior himself, that is, God incarnate.*

DIVISIONS OF THEOLOGY

There is no question that this is systematic theologizing, as intellectually satisfying as the design of the thirteenth-century gothic cathedrals, great statements of faith that they are. Both fill us with awe and respect today, even though our tastes have changed and we look for other ways to God. In Aquinas's system, dogmatic theology and moral theology appear together, implying a desirable synthesis of faith and life, and providing the principles for it. In his *Summa* the former category includes also attention to questions, like God's existence, faith and revelation, that today would be attended to separately as fundamental theology; we would find there a sacramental theology as well. Aquinas's moral theology would suggest also principles of spiritual development that would today be classed as ascetical theology.

All of these content categories of theology, of course, could be treated not so much speculatively, by the logical development of principles as Aquinas's scholastic method does, as historically (or positively), showing what the Bible and the Fathers or the magisterium of the Church ("Denzinger theology") had to say on a range of topics within each category. We shall look at a range of contemporary methods of theology in Chapter 12.

The Scholastics in their systems were not concerned with what today is called practical theology. This includes attention to education in the faith through preaching and catechesis (pastoral theology also a name for this) and to living the Christian life in today's society.

DIVISIONS OF THEOLOGY

by content	by method
• fundamental theology	• historical, positive theology
• systematic theology	biblical
dogmatic	patristic
moral	magisterial
sacramental	• speculative theology
• practical, pastoral theology	

Theology can also be looked at from the viewpoint of its locus, whether the pulpits of the Fathers, the monasteries, the schools and universities, the seminary, the library, the marketplace, not to mention a range of cultural contexts within which men and women theologize. Today we are less concerned with system and logic than with relevance and authenticity; we want our theology to speak to, and make sense of, the real world in which we live.

SOME FURTHER READING

It is a worthwhile endeavor to look in the Scriptures for some pattern, some meaningful matrix that will allow us to make sense of all the disparate data about God's plan for all things that they relay to us in such fascinating diversity. We have mentioned before the (deutero)pauline pattern of "the mystery of Christ" that Paul and his disciples found helpful, especially but not solely its ecclesial dimension affecting the admission of Gentiles into that plan, and as well cosmic, historical, biblical, and personal dimensions. In Jesus' mouth the term *basileia* (occurring just 100 times in our Gospels, by comparison with perhaps one occurrence of *ecclesia*, "church") serves as a similar significant umbrella term for the whole series of values that God wants implemented in the world ("kingdom" is not such an accurate translation) and that Jesus sets about proclaiming and inaugurating. My *Jesus and the Mystery of Christ* looks at both from this point of view.

Jewish theology beyond the Bible, and especially the scholarly and rabbinic commentary since the Exile, should be an object of our study, especially as it had a formative influence on the New Testament. Paul's use of and debate about *sophia*, "wisdom," for example, as in *1 Cor* 1–2, has this body of teaching in mind. The Talmud is accessible in books like A. Cohen's *Everyman's Talmud*, New York: Shocken, 1975, and that prolific Jewish scholar Jacob Neusner's *Invitation to the Talmud*, New York: Harper and Row, 1973. The article by Leland J. White is helpful, "Midrash: a key to the meaning of the Scriptures," *PACE* (*Professional Approaches for Christian Educators*) 17 (1986) 81–85. The classic work on the biblical interpretation of Fathers and medievals has long been Beryl Smalley's *The Study of the Bible in the Middle Ages*, 3rd edn, Oxford: Blackwell, 1983.

System has never been a feature of the East, especially with its accent on the apophatic (as distinct from kataphatic) tradition in theology—that is, on the view (with which Aquinas too opens the *Summa*) that we can know and say less rather than more about God. We have mentioned before the Greek respect for divine transcendence—*aphatos*, "unspeakable," being a habitual term in Fathers like Chrysostom. So, apart perhaps from John Damascene's *Exposition of the Orthodox Doctrine* in the eighth century that closed the patristic period in the East, there has been no Greek summa. The work of the Greek Fathers tended instead to be defensive, condemning aberrations from the truth rather than outlining its totality. Australian Orthodox theologian John Chryssavgis outlines the different approaches well in his "Sources of patristic theology," *Phronema* 3 (1988) 21–30. In the century after Aquinas there arose in the East the great Gregory Palamas with his work on a favorite oriental theme, deification of humanity and nature as a whole; but it does not bear the Western emphasis on rationality. In fact, at the Council of Florence, the last attempt to achieve a reconciliation of East and West, in the fifteenth century, a Greek bishop expostulated on mention of Aquinas and his use of Aristotle's philosophy, "A fig for your Aristotle! We have Basil."

The *Summa Theologiae* of Aquinas has, of course, been translated into all languages, even if today it has become a reference rather than the classroom manual it once was. The practice of theologians developing a complete *summa* has not continued, though great Protestant and Catholic examples exist from theologians like Karl Barth. The equally prolific Karl Rahner developed a looser series of treatises now collected in English in more than a score of volumes entitled *Theological Investigations*. The market for theology is less the medieval "school" than the more casual (lay) reader in the world. Two famous Roman theologians, Z. Alszeghy and M. Flick, in their *Introductory Theology*, Eng. trans, London: Sheed and Ward, 1982, maintain:

> *The criticism most frequently raised against the theological science of our time is precisely the lack of a new synthesis, adapted to the present state of ecclesial consciousness, to present-day knowledge of theological sources and to the contemporary cultural situation* (90).

Theology, as is suggested above, is capable of division in various ways: content, method, locus, perspective, tradition, religion. Brennan Hill examines many of these divisions in his part of *Faith, Religion and Theology*. Richard McBrien, who has produced a modern manual, if not theological *summa*, in *Catholicism*, rev. edn, Melbourne: CollinsDove, 1993, deals in its Introduction with divisions of theology.

EXERCISES IN THEOLOGY

1. Has the desire for system in your approach to faith ever been a concern for you? Does the Bible, for instance, present itself to you as a meaningful whole, or just a bewildering series of largely unrelated documents? How can the problem be resolved (in other words, how adequate is your biblical theology)?

2. Look at the new *Catechism of the Catholic Church.* Note its careful structure (that of the Trent catechism). Does that sort of overall systematic treatment (as in your childhood catechism, perhaps) bring satisfaction? Does any unease remain (the Pope in introducing it, for instance, admits the need for local adaptation)?

3. From the documents of Vatican II read the decree on priestly formation #16 on theological formation. Can you see how, in typically Roman style, the age-old endorsement of medieval systems like Aquinas's is repeated but nuanced? Which are now seen to be the key values in theological education? Have you enjoyed them?

8

Sources and traditions

The faith of each of us is a response to our experience of God's word and action. Insofar as it is Christian faith, God's word and action comes to us preeminently in Jesus. The experience that gives rise to faith is both personal and communitarian. I have experienced God in my life in various ways, and I share in the community's experiences, especially those foundational experiences like the Paschal Mystery. Remember Paul: he had a most memorable encounter with the risen Lord, and yet felt the need to be inserted into those foundational experiences of the community of which he had not initially been part. Only then could he speak of what is "of first importance" to the community and introduce others to it.

BACK TO THE SOURCES

The Scriptures, creeds and systems that we have studied so far have attempted to take us back to the sources of our faith. When the worshipper with first fruits in hand approached the shrine in the Deuteronomist's Israel, his ritual began with the apparently irrelevant reference to the time when "my father was a wandering Aramean" who went down into Egypt. His credo was aimed at linking his harvest offering into that significant story, which lay at the basis of his faith in a God who acts. Christian liturgy and sacraments do likewise today, because our faith springs from those sources.

My own faith journey has been blessed with opportunities to appreciate those means of return to the sources, scriptural and doctrinal and systematic. In the course of being introduced to the system of Aquinas—an invaluable formative opportunity—I recall our being diverted by the retort of our mentor, an excellent Thomist, to trends just then appearing at the Vatican Council. (It was a heady time to be studying in Rome.) "*Back to the sources,*" he snorted, "the cry of every heresy from the beginning!" For him the path to the sources of our faith need reach only as far as the great medieval systematizers, especially Aquinas, who brought together in orderly fashion all that was worthwhile from ages closer to the foundational events. A more enlightened confrere of his, Chenu, would admit:

People have come to perceive the limitations of reason when brought face to face with the Christian mystery and to realize the gulf separating religious experience from the categories of philosophy . . .

The return to the writings and to the true spirit of the Fathers has done much to clear the air and to revive the sense of mystery in theological studies. This is something which system-building, if pursued for its own sake, tends to diminish but which the reading of the Gospels nourishes and fosters.

It has therefore been a blessing for me to proceed from that systematic basis to further scriptural and patristic study. For one thing, it has put me in touch with Eastern as well as Western forms of Christian life and theology. We in the West do not share the accent on mystery and divine transcendence, on the deification of the human being, on the role of the Spirit, on healing rather than fall that emerges from the worship and theology of the East. Western, Roman forms of worship, models of Church, doctrinal expressions and styles of theologizing do not exhaust the totality of means of response to the sources of faith. Our map of "The World of the Fathers" (p. 38 above) demonstrates clearly the purchase that Eastern centers of Christian life had on Christendom in early centuries. It explains why the patriarchates and ecumenical councils were to be found east of the Italian peninsula. The schism of East and West in the eleventh century deprived us of this sense of diversity; we tend to think now in a monochrome Western fashion, and are the poorer for it.

THE ROLE OF TRADITION

What the Scriptures, the creeds, the Fathers and our forms of worship allow us to do is to revisit the *magnalia Dei*, the wonderful words and actions of our God who acts—in Jesus. They transmit to us experiences of the foundational communities in which we did not directly share, but in which we must be participants if our faith is to be Christian faith. Our Christian faith is nourished by this transmission, this *tradition*

(Latin *tradere*, "hand on") in its various forms, as other religious faiths would be nourished by their forms of tradition—Jewish faith by the festivals of Judaism, for example. Like a Jew's participation in a Passover meal, a Christian's celebration of the Eucharist is a return to the sources of Christianity—not just a recollection but *anamnesis*, the reenactment enjoined by Jesus at the Supper allowing us to appropriate what is recalled by word and action.

Religious tradition, and specifically Christian tradition, thus takes many forms, not all taken advantage of equally by all communities. All rely on the *scriptural* form of transmission of the foundational experiences. Reliance on *doctrinal* tradition, however, characterizes the Roman community in particular, to the extent that "tradition" can mean

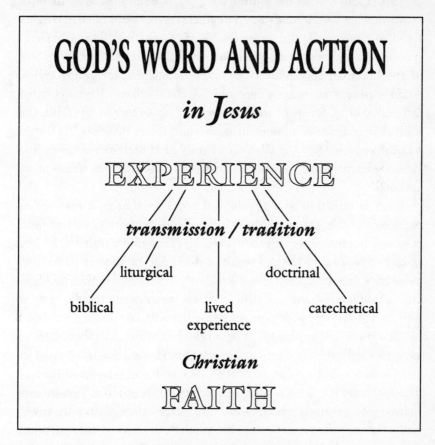

GOD'S WORD AND ACTION

in Jesus

EXPERIENCE

transmission / tradition

liturgical   doctrinal

biblical   lived   catechetical
                   experience

Christian

FAITH

Experience, tradition, faith

this form alone or at least preeminently—as in this statement from the new Catechism:

> *Tradition is to be distinguished from the various*
> *theological, disciplinary, liturgical, or devotional*
> *traditions, born in the local churches over time. These are*
> *the particular forms, adapted to different places and*
> *times, in which the great Tradition is expressed. In the*
> *light of Tradition, these traditions can be retained,*
> *modified or even abandoned under the guidance of the*
> *Church's magisterium (#83).*

Liturgical tradition we have already spoken of. The *catechetical* tradition of Christianity, whereby sound doctrine is communicated in faith education, has been strong since the earliest times, exemplified in Origen, Cyril of Jerusalem and some works of Augustine. The *homiletic* (preaching) tradition represents also a continuous line of faith formation of the Christian people involving characteristic oral forms and styles, again stronger in some communities than others. Perhaps most influential of all forms of tradition is *lived experience* of the faith, the kind of rounded transmission of beliefs and values that only life within a faithfilled unit like the Christian family or church can achieve; it is virtually irreplaceable, as we acknowledge if we see the dire effects of its absence.

Such is tradition as a theological *process*—that is, a manner of catching us up in the community's experience that promotes our faith response and that we scrutinize in theology. Tradition can also be looked upon as a *product*, as the end result of doctrinal tradition in particular, as we have seen from the *Catechism* above. The word can thus be used, and is frequently used in Catholic statements, despite the decision at Vatican II to reject the notion, as correlative with or even in opposition to "Scripture" in the phrase "Scripture and Tradition," as though these were two independent founts of revelation. (Pope John intervened in the Council's first session to order a new text and new commission.) The distinction is as inadequate as "carrots and vegetables," the former being more precisely one form of the latter rather than a different entity—hence the Council's unease (though the text of its statement *Dei Verbum* still carries the phrase: not all decisions on the Council floor reached the scribes!). This is a phrase not found among other Western or Eastern groups; Orthodox theologian John Meyendorff speaks for the latter:

> *Scripture, while complete in itself, presupposes Tradition, not as an addition, but as a milieu in which it becomes understandable and meaningful . . . There cannot be, therefore, any question about "two sources" of Revelation.*

TRADITION, TRADITION AND TRADITIONS

The Catholic tendency to speak of Scripture as though it is not a form of the community's transmissional processes derives from that vast reaction in late medieval Christendom against some *traditions* and even some abuses in forms of tradition (of which the *Catechism* speaks) that we know as the Reformation. Exaggeration and imbalance in medieval expressions of piety, undue sacramental realism and loss of a Paschal perspective in the liturgy, doctrinal excesses in the areas of grace and forgiveness, a growing gap between vernacular languages and Latin scriptures, departure in Church structures from the spirit of the Gospels—all these deficiencies in the community's life of faith prompted a "protest" and call for reform. A German Bible translator and Augustinian theologian, Martin Luther, was in a position in the early sixteenth century to swing this "Protestant" movement behind his own preference for the scriptural form of tradition, giving rise to the Reformation's catchcry *scriptura sola*. Contemporary new learning was also promoting and making possible a return to the sources through the Bible. Luther's polemic laid the groundwork for the unfortunate dichotomy between forms of tradition:

> *We do not condemn the doctrines of men just because they are the doctrines of men, for we would gladly put up with them. But we condemn them because they are contrary to the Gospel and the Scriptures. While the Scriptures liberate consciences and forbid that they be taken captive by the doctrines of men, these doctrines of men captivate the conscience anyhow. This conflict between the Scriptures and the doctrines of men we cannot reconcile . . .*

> *It is not necessary that there should be everywhere the*
> *same traditions of men, or the same rites and ceremonies*
> *devised by men.*

In Switzerland John Calvin lent his support to this superiority of the scriptural over the doctrinal forms of Christian tradition:

> *Let this be a firm principle: No other word is to be held as*
> *the Word of God, and given place as such in the Church,*
> *than what is contained first in the Law and the Prophets,*
> *then in the writings of the apostles; and the only*
> *authorized way of teaching in the Church is by the*
> *prescription and standard of his Word.*

So for the Reformation the way back to the sources for Christians is through the Bible alone; it is the supreme form of tradition, and all others are superfluous or deficient. Scripture is the *norma normans*, the rule to be applied to all others. "The distinguishing mark of the Reformation and its disciples," says modern Protestant scholar Ernst Käsemann, " is the exclusive particle, the word 'alone,' " *scriptura sola*. In a kneejerk reaction—unbalanced as such reactions often are—the Catholic counter-reform claimed to have both "Scripture and tradition." That inadequate distinction was intended to refer to those other forms of transmission of foundational experiences that the community enjoys to nourish its faith. Orthodox theology less polemically admits the possibility of decay in traditional forms while asserting their value for Church life:

> *The one Holy Tradition, which constitutes the self-identity*
> *of the Church through the ages and is the organic and*
> *visible expression of the life of the Spirit in the Church, is*
> *not to be confused with the inevitable, often creative and*
> *positive, sometimes sinful, and always relative*
> *accumulation of human traditions in the historical*
> *Church.*
>
> J. MEYENDORFF, *LIVING TRADITION*

TRADITION AND CHURCH

Underlying the theology of tradition and the role of the Scriptures in particular is a theology of Church. Käsemann can assert with obvious support from Luther and Calvin that "it will not be unfair if we sum up the ideal of piety among Protestant congregations in the formula: every man sitting down with his Bible in front of him! Undoubtedly this conception does point towards the Church as the hearing and obeying community." While this model of Church and its related model of herald find a place in Catholic and Orthodox ecclesiology, these communities and (to judge from statements by the Anglican-Roman Catholic International Commission [ARCIC]) the Church of England thinks of Church more roundly as community of life, *koinonia*. In such ecclesiology the divine offer of life reaches us in other ways than solely the scriptural—preeminently in the celebration of the Eucharist, for instance. The mystery of the Church, as Paul says of the mystery of Christ (*Eph* 3.10), is multi-dimensioned, many-faceted, *polypoikilos*.

SOME FURTHER READING

It has been suggested above that, to enjoy a comprehensively Christian vision, we should acquaint ourselves also with the outlines of Eastern and specifically Orthodox theology and traditions. An easy introduction is provided by L. Cross, *Eastern Christianity: The Byzantine Tradition*, Sydney: Dwyer, 1988. Yves Congar has devoted much of his theological energies to reminding the West of Eastern theology and the diversity of Christian traditions to which the East makes its proper contribution. His earlier thoughts on *Tradition and Traditions* he includes with further such recommendations in *Diversity and Communion* (1982), Eng. trans, Mystic: Twenty-Third Publications, 1985. Better still, read today's Orthodox theologians like John Zizioulas, Kallistos Ware, Georges Florovsky, Basil Krivocheine, Sergius Bulgakov, Dumitru Staniloae, John Chryssavgis, and John Meyendorff, whose *Living Tradition. Orthodox Witness in the Contemporary World*, Crestwood NY: St Vladimir Seminary Press, 1978, we quoted from above. Another helpful summary is Alexander Schmemann's *Church, World, Mission. Reflections on Orthodoxy in the West*, Crestwood: SVS, 1979.

Though tradition is a characteristically (if often misunderstood) Catholic notion, the World Council of Churches at the Montreal conference of its Faith and Order Commission in 1963 studied the notion under various aspects. Like Rome, this WCC conference defined

Tradition *as product* as "the revelation of God and the gift which he has made of himself in Christ, his presence in the life of the Church." This Tradition is actualized in tradition *as process*, "in the preaching of the Word, in the administration of the sacraments and worship, in Christian teaching and theology, and in mission and witness to Christ by the lives of the members of the Church." That excellent explanation of the varied transmission of the Church's foundational experiences might not satisfy a vintage Protestant like Käsemann, nor the scribes at Vatican II who still pushed for two sources of revelation under the tag "Scripture and tradition," but it does justice to our thinking above.

Martin Luther, once represented as a monster in some Catholic literature, has in these ecumenical days been rehabilitated and credit given him for his promotion of the Scriptures in the vernacular. This work is nobly continued today through the Bible Societies, who have translated them into more than 2000 languages and seek tirelessly and generously to have them distributed everywhere. "Luther against the background of the history of biblical interpretation," *Interpretation* 37 (1983) 229–39, is an interesting article by S. Hendrix. For Luther's theology generally we can turn to the volumes of his collected *Works*, ed. E. Bachmann, Philadelphia: Fortress Press; the quotation above comes from his essay "On avoiding the doctrines of men" in vol. 35. The piece from John Calvin is from volume 21 of his great work, *Institutes of the Christian Religion*, Philadelphia: Westminster. Ernst Käsemann, a fine New Testament scholar, includes the essay from which we quoted, "Thoughts about the present controversy on scriptural interpretation," in his *New Testament Questions of Today*, Eng. trans, London: SCM, 1969.

EXERCISES IN THEOLOGY

1. To my shame, I was brought up in a (typically Catholic?) nonbiblical environment, at home, in church, at school; we would speak scornfully of "Bible-bashers." Fortunately I had opportunities to overcome this prejudice. How scriptural have been your upbringing, schooling, professional formation, reading, teaching, praying?

2. Vatican II (*Dei Verbum 21*) speaks glowingly—though perhaps more as ideal than fact—of the Church constantly offering the bread of life from the table both of the Word of God and of the body of Christ. Do you see evidence that Christian formation has become equally scriptural as eucharistic? Should it? What steps need to be taken?

3. Being human in their development, all forms of tradition, i.e., transmission of our community's foundational experiences, require periodic reform, restatement, fresh expression. Have you lived through such processes of reform—of the liturgy, for instance, or catechesis, or doctrinal formulation? Can you see need of further reform?

9

Theology's sources under criticism

I sometimes drive on an expressway that passes the outskirts of a big industrial city. If you're not concentrating totally on the road ahead, your eye may be caught by a large, barn-door size sign deliberately mounted at the bottom of his backyard by some householder as a manifesto for passing motorists to see. It reads simply and starkly:

THE
BIBLE
ALONE.

It always strikes me as a wonderful statement of faith and theology both, and I generally remark to anyone traveling with me, "Ah, the Reformation lives!"

THE BIBLE, THEOLOGY'S ONLY SOURCE?

It is not a credal statement from the seven ecumenical councils that we studied in Chapter 6, though it is close to that article of the Niceno-Constantinopolitan creed, "He has spoken through the prophets (i.e., biblical authors)." I suppose we can say we have faith in the Bible; but it is more a theological conviction being expressed here of the priority, even unicity, of this form of tradition of the Christian community's foundational experiences. So if the Bible is not a source of our faith, in the way that the Paschal Mystery is, it can and often is said to be a source of our theologizing. We turn to it to find where the early theologian Paul divined that this mystery is "of first importance" for his new community (and ours), as the Deuteronomist's text has the worshipper point to Exodus and Conquest as the basis of his faith. That is why Vatican II suggests that the scriptural tradition of Christianity is a more fundamental source and guide for theologians than medieval systems.

But, of course, Paul also speaks to the Corinthians of their celebration of the Paschal Mystery in eucharistic form. Deuteronomy's worshipper too—perforce, considering the technology of the time, when texts were rare—was celebrating in cult those foundational events (*Dt* 26). Neither could have been content with text alone as a source of their theological convictions. The earlier chapter 6 of *Deuteronomy* in fact reflects lived experience and the catechetical tradition at work as well, the child and parent engaging in a question and answer process of faith education around the table at festival time. Early council Fathers obviously thought that the Scriptures needed the supplement of precise formulation, which aberrant theological schools failed to find in the Bible that they all quoted. In short, for some Christians, "alone" is not a term they could append to the Bible in listing the source of their theologizing and religious education. Another way of putting it is that there are more "languages of faith" available for expressing what we believe, which the community (at least most Christian communities, and many others) in practice take advantage of.

In the wake of the Reformation, however, many could accept the Bible "alone." Australian novelist Tim Winton tells of his youth in an evangelical church:

> *The Scriptures were really influential in my upbringing. Our tradition was very non-conformist, very civilian, if I can put it that way. Anti-intellectual, anti-representative, anti-professional. There was no ornamentation, no real sense of form or liturgy, no notion of sacrament, aside from baptism, which was very definitely full-immersion baptism. A pretty austere tradition. Protestants still protesting, still reacting to the idea of embroidery. An effort to get back to the Source, and the only pure source of revelation was in the Scriptures . . .*
>
> *But later I realized that something was missing. The plainness and austerity weren't simply a discipline, but a blindness to mystery, a fear of Bigness and Beauty. My tradition was in the grip of the spiritual/physical divide. In the end my own instincts won out.*

(The interview with novelist Tim Winton by Howard Willis is reproduced with permission of the publishers of *Eureka Street*, September 1994.)

SACRED TEXTS UNDER CHALLENGE

Yet the austerity of which Tim Winton complains and had to supplement, multitudes of other Christians since the Reformation found encouraging,

especially when compared with Latin and oriental exuberance in worship
and Church life generally. What could constitute a more fundamental
questioning of their faith was the challenge that came to be mounted
against the very texts they had chosen as source in preference to liturgy,
sacrament, mystery generally.

The sacred texts on which tannaim and rabbis pondered in the wake
of the Exile and which they embroidered with their talmudic styles of
commentary were so esteemed as word of God that both oral Torah and
written Torah were thought to have been communicated on Sinai. To
subject them to normal literary scrutiny, or *criticism* (from the Greek
word for "evaluation"), would be improper. The early Church thought
likewise of these texts. Jesus and his contemporaries clearly took at face
value a story like *Jonah* that we would see as a later fictionalized satire
on Israel's prophetic tradition (*Mt* 12.39–41). The Fathers in almost all
cases studied the Bible without the aid of knowledge of biblical languages.
Augustine had no good grasp of Greek. Chrysostom, Greek-speaking
himself, had no Hebrew to help his commentary on *Genesis*, nor critical
skills to allow him to recognize diversity of sources in his material; when
he came to the close of the first creation narrative at *Genesis* 2.4 and
saw another list of created things beginning, he naively remarked to his
congregation:

> *The Holy Spirit, after all, in his foreknowledge of future
> events wishes to prevent anyone's being able to engage in
> controversy later on, and in opposition to Sacred Scripture
> to set notions from their own reasoning against the
> dogmas of the Church; so now again, after teaching us the
> order of created things . . . accordingly once again he
> makes mention of all the items one by one so as to stop the
> unbridled tongue of people spoiling to make a show of
> their shamelessness.*

HOMILY 12 ON *GENESIS*

We have seen the medievals' lack of understanding of the true nature of
the biblical texts as well, though they found other ways to provide a
coherent theological perspective.

Luther and—by a happy coincidence—the invention of printing put
vernacular translations of the Scriptures into the hands of people who

had previously depended on preacher and painter and sculptor for acquaintance with the biblical stories. Käsemann's individual believer "sitting with Bible open in front of him" became the model of faith formation, and remained so for ages—until a whole new crisis developed in the form of biblical criticism. The reliability of these records of the faith of the fathers was thrown into question: could the Bible itself be believed?

THE IMPACT OF RATIONALIST CRITICISM

It was just a matter of time before advances in the natural sciences and the rationalist Age of Enlightenment focused on religious literatures, as on ancient literatures generally. Archaeological and geographical discoveries in Palestine called into question the accuracy of biblical statement. In one three-month period in 1838 more biblical sites were located than in all the time since historian Eusebius in the fourth century. As early as 1678 the priest Richard Simon (once Protestant) had by dint of literary and historical analysis questioned the Mosaic authorship of the Pentateuch. Even Rome reacted by placing his work on the Index of forbidden books; but his emphasis on the lateness of our Hebrew texts and the evidence of many authorial hands at work in the Pentateuch gained support in the following century or so. Thus arose the historical–critical method of approaching the Bible, with its emphasis on change and development, associated in the nineteenth century with the names of scholars like Julius Wellhausen and Bernard Duhm.

The impulse to apply to the New Testament as well historical–critical principles also came from Richard Simon. Scholars continued in the eighteenth and nineteenth centuries to examine the Gospels, previously taken as simple factual biographies of Jesus, for mythological and dogmatic embellishments and for evidence of cultural and religious ideas stemming from Judaism and Hellenism. Paul's chronological priority was recognized; even Luther had admitted, "In the Scholastics I lost Christ, but found him again in Paul"—not in the Gospels. Lives of Jesus based on the Gospels were shown to lack adequate historical foundation. Discrepancies in the various Gospel accounts were highlighted, and sources hunted; the historicity of John was virtually rejected. By the beginning of the twentieth century skepticism about the Gospel versions of Jesus' life was widespread (except among Catholics, who in their Counter-Reformation mentality had not kept up with scholarly developments).

DEATH OF THE HISTORICAL JESUS

The *coup de grace* to evangelical Christian theologians invoking the Gospels as their prime source came with the form criticism developed by German scholars Martin Dibelius and Rudolf Bultmann in the wake of the "Great War." This form-critical method concentrated on the preexisting forms—parables, miracle stories and so on—which the evangelists assembled as mere compilers. Influenced by the dispiriting defeat of the German people, by Heidegger's existentialist philosophy and by the development in historiography of a positivism that admitted only historical fact, Bultmann, professor in Marburg, was also a good Lutheran. He therefore prized the New Testament, but to rest on the life of the historical Jesus would also be a betrayal of the Lutheran principle of "by faith alone." So he had no difficulty in accepting that the Gospel narratives present us with a mythical overlay, a figurative manner of presentation arising from the biblical worldview which is not our worldview. We must remove that overlay, or "demythologize" the Gospels, if we are properly to interpret them.

> *Critical investigation shows that the whole tradition about Jesus which appears in the three Synoptic Gospels is composed of a series of layers which can on the whole be clearly distinguished . . .*
> *By means of this critical analysis an oldest layer is determined, though it can be marked off with only relative exactness. Naturally we have no absolute assurance that the exact words of this oldest layer were really spoken by Jesus. There is a possibility that the contents of this oldest layer are also the result of a complicated historical process which we can no longer trace.*
> *Of course, the doubt as to whether Jesus really existed is unfounded and not worth refutation. No sane person can doubt that Jesus stands as founder behind the historical movement whose first distinct stage is represented by the*

> *oldest Palestinian community. But how far that*
> *community preserved an objectively true picture of him*
> *and his message is another question.*
>   *JESUS AND THE WORD* (1926; ET 1934)

Scholarly skepticism of this kind, religiously motivated though it may have been, was devastating for believers and theologians who pinned their convictions on Bible alone. The pivotal tradition of Christianity, the biblical text, could not be depended on. The authenticity of its Old Testament authors had been abolished along with the factual character of salvation history and Gospel, and in their place stood myth. The very life of Jesus could not be plotted with certainty; there was no guarantee he had ever spoken the words attributed to him.

Responses to Bultmann's work and to the historical–critical method thus applied to Old Testament and to Gospels were various. For some, agnosticism was the only possibility: we can now know nothing of God and his plan for us in Jesus. Another world war only deepened this skepticism, resulting in the "God is dead" movement. For others the reaction was to reject out of hand the "findings" of scholars and go back to "The Fundamentals," in the title of a seminal work in the United States. "Give us that old time religion" became the catchcry of such fundamentalists, as the movie *Inherit the Wind* dramatizes. Among the scholars themselves, especially in England but also in Germany, there was a different, more positive response, sifting out the less radical of the form critics' proposals and finding something to proceed with. Even among Bultmann's former students a "post-Bultmannian" reaction moved in that direction. Postmodern historiography assisted this movement by allowing for a subjective element in the writing of history, so that evangelists could be seen legitimately as theologians rather than simply recorders of fact about Jesus.

FUNDAMENTALISM AND ITS ALTERNATIVES

Fredric March and Spencer Tracy in that early movie about the Scopes "Monkey Trial" illustrated well the opposing views in the fundamentalist debate. It concerned not simply the interpretation of biblical texts and doctrines contained in them, like the creation of the world. As novelist Tim Winton remarked of his evangelical upbringing, the movement generally was anti-intellectual, anti-professional, putting physical and spiritual at odds, mistrusting Bigness and Beauty and mystery—and, of course, rationalist scholars had to carry much of the blame for this extreme reaction. In theological terms, fundamentalism is a failure to accept fully the Incarnation: the historical incarnation in that we thus prefer to bypass normal ways to God and achieve a "hotline" relationship (as in Pentecostalist sects), and the scriptural incarnation in that we refuse the evidence of change and development in texts, diversity of authorship, inculturated attitudes, an outdated cosmology. "It was good enough for Moses," chanted Fredric March's supporters in the movie, "and it's good enough for me." The emphasis on reading the Bible was on fact, not truth; inerrancy was the prime effect of divine inspiration— and Spencer Tracy showed how illogical that attitude could be.

The Catholic community was largely unaffected by the wave of fundamentalist material emanating from publishing houses like Garland Publishing, Inc., New York. Caught in their Counter-Reformation nonbiblical time warp, they were unlikely to have access to a Bible, which was in any case before this century a large, unwieldy volume, opening with a prayer against the infection of private interpretation. A change of direction was signaled just a century ago with an encyclical from Pope Leo XIII in 1893, *Providentissimus Deus*. It cautiously recommended a greater knowledge of Scripture, largely for apologetic purposes, and joined forces with fundamentalists in insisting on the inerrancy of the Bible. Gradually provision in the Catholic community was made for some minimal scriptural formation of the clergy, for example through establishment of a Roman Biblical Commission. But it was fifty years before Pope Pius XII with his encyclical *Divino Afflante Spiritu* in 1943 wholeheartedly encouraged Catholic biblical scholars to catch up with the best findings of their Protestant counterparts in the area of biblical criticism. A further fifty years saw statements by the Biblical Commission on the Gospels (1964), the Bible and Christology (1984), and ways to interpret the Bible generally (1993). While the community has still to throw off its fundamentalism totally, better theological education is introducing it not only to historical-critical criticism—the fruits of archaeology, textual criticism, language study, literary and form criticism—but also to a range of other approaches to the text.

Methods and approaches in biblical interpretation

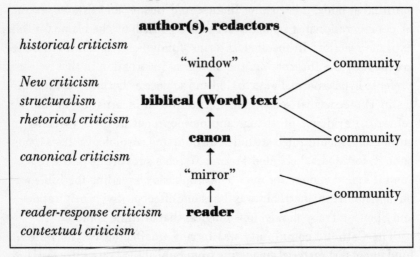

These more recent methods, the New criticism, suggest that we read the text not just as a window on the world of the author but as a mirror reflecting a world into which the reader is invited—reading the Exodus story not just as historical event but as liberating experience for us too. Our responses as readers within certain cultural and human situations are of relevance, too; men and women will respond differently to a text like *Judges* 19, for instance. Canonical criticism suggests that we read individual books within the canon of Old or New Testament or Bible as a whole, as part of the community for whom the text was composed—though the Word or text has spoken to a series of faith communities.

Adoption of such new hermeneutical approaches would draw a dividing line between fundamentalists and others for whom "The Bible Alone" remained the sole theological source. Ultimately, however, the question comes down to one's understanding of the role of theology within the community, unless Bible and theology are to be ends in themselves. The new *Catechism of the Catholic Church* reminds Christians that they are not members of "a Religion of the Book" (#108), that it is a living Word to which they commit themselves in faith. (The corollary is, of course, that a doctrinal form of tradition like the *CCC* should likewise not become *the* book of this religion). The community's self-understanding determines the role that theology takes and its sources.

SOME FURTHER READING

The history of biblical criticism is well documented. Any Introduction to the Bible, Old or New Testament (such as those we cite in Chapter 14) will trace key developments and figures and works. A useful summary is found in the chapters on "Modern Old/New Testament Criticism" in the *New Jerome Biblical Commentary*. For an understanding of the forms of biblical criticism, the series *Guides to Biblical Scholarship* on both Old and New Testaments published by Fortress Press, Philadelphia, is helpful, including titles like *Historical–Critical Method* (E. Krentz), *What is Redaction Criticism?* (N. Perrin) and *Form Criticism of the Old Testament* (G. M. Tucker).

Just as the impact of Martin Luther's ideas was reinforced by contemporary societal, religious and technological developments, so Rudolf Bultmann's call to demythologize the Gospels was reinforced by historical and philosophical developments in post-World War Europe. It was also correspondingly nuanced by changing attitudes to historiography that saw historians' role less as recorders than interpreters. The evangelists could then be acknowledged as individual theologians not confined to a factual biography of Jesus but aiming at a theological presentation of him in terms of Old Testament patterns and the needs of their own communities. Bultmann's views (printed here with permission) were contained in his *Jesus and the Word* (1926), Eng.trans., New York: Charles Scribner's Sons, 1934, and *The History of the Synoptic Tradition*, 2nd edn (1931), Eng. trans., Oxford: Blackwell, 1968. British scholarship of the period, in the person of scholars like Vincent Taylor, R. H. Lightfoot and C. H. Dodd, was more conservative and took only the best conclusions of the German form critics.

Fundamentalism is a political, economic and religious phenomenon that continues in today's world unabated; in religious matters we can distinguish its biblical, doctrinal and charismatic manifestations. Christianity is not alone in bearing the marks. James Barr has done a thorough study: *Fundamentalism*, London: SCM, 1978. Also helpful are: M. Boys, "Fundamentalism," *PACE* 11 (1981); R. McBrien, "Teaching Catholicism today: the challenge of Fundamentalism," *PACE* 16 (1986); E. LaVerdiere, "Fundamentalism," *The Bible Today* 21

(1983), 5–11; J. A. Sanders, "Fundamentalism and the Church: Theological crisis for mainline Protestants," *Biblical Theology Bulletin*, 18 (1988), 43–9. While associated with Bible-belt Protestantism in particular, it is to be found in Catholic circles, if only because of the lag in critical studies remarked on above. Even a conservative body like Rome's Congregation for the Doctrine of the Faith has warned against taking Church statements without due regard for their relativity and historical conditioning:

> *Difficulties arise from the historical condition that affects the expression of revelation. With regard to this historical condition, it must first be observed that the meaning of the pronouncements of faith depends partly upon the expressive power of the language used at a certain point in time and in particular circumstances. Moreover, it sometimes happens that some dogmatic truth is first expressed incompletely (but not falsely), and at a later date, when considered in a broader context of faith or human knowledge, it receives a fuller and more perfect expression.*

MYSTERIUM ECCLESIAE (1973)

The National Conference of Catholic Bishops in the US also released a Statement on Biblical Fundamentalism in 1987; for the bishops "fundamentalism indicates a person's general approach to life which is typified by unyielding adherence to rigid doctrinal and ideological positions."

The text of biblical encyclicals can be found in English in *Rome and the Study of Scripture*, rev. edn, St Meinrad: Grail Publications, 1962. In Vatican II's *Dei Verbum* on the Bible the Pontifical Biblical Commission's 1964 Instruction on the composition of the Gospels is summarized, including the most positive findings of previous (Protestant) scholarship on the evangelists. The 1993 PBC Instruction, *The Interpretation of the Bible in the Church*, a lengthy and thorough statement of modern exegetical and hermeneutical methods and approaches (and the fundamentalism that arises from their neglect), has been published by St Paul Publications, Boston.

EXERCISES IN THEOLOGY

1. Is "The Bible Alone" an axiom in your religious community? If not, do you know people for whom it is? Do you feel competent to discuss the sources of theology with them, perhaps suggesting that other ways to make sense of faith are available? If not, what further resourcing do you require?

2. Do you feel under threat if someone applies critical approaches to the Bible? Does "criticism" carry negative overtones for you in this regard? How secure do you feel if even a conservative authority, like the Pontifical Biblical Commission or the Catechism, recommends critical reading of these ancient but fundamental texts? Would you class yourself "fundamentalist" in scriptural or doctrinal matters?

3. Often one hears laments about "changes in the Church." What lies behind such laments? What can be done to bring people to accept change and development as natural and necessary in Church life and statement?

10

Theology and Church

When in his recent book *Crossing the Threshold of Hope* Karol Wojtyla asks himself the question, "If God exists, why is he in hiding?", his being on the seat of Peter as John Paul II no more heightens the urgency and anguish of the question than does Job's place "among the ashes" as he poses the same conundrum. Faith is originally and ultimately a personal and even solitary response to a revealing God, as Jesus knew in his agony. Käsemann's version of the Protestant "ideal of piety," every man sitting down with his Bible in front of him, endorses the same personal relationship that is faith.

A FAITH COMMUNITY

Yet we have seen the peril, not simply the anguish, that such solitary individualism constitutes for the believer. The author of *The Babylonian Theodicy* never did receive an answer to his bewilderment about his lot in life. Job had his day in court even though his community of friends were ignored by the Judge as purveyors of a discredited theology. He himself was still left—after a rebuke for endeavoring to pry into divine transcendence—to accept in faith that human wisdom pales before divine Wisdom, in which suffering mysteriously makes sense. The mystery remains, as it can for believers with Bible open before them.

We made the point in Chapter 1 that faith is not religion, and unnecessary confusion on this point can also cause heartache. My faith relationship, and my children's, may survive a breakdown in religious practice and even departure from a particular religious group in which I had been accustomed to celebrate the sources of my faith. Yet, as a Christian, I need the guarantee of participation in a Christian community to be sure that my relationship with the God who comes to me in Jesus is a valid Christian faith. Only then could Paul, the believer turned Christian, determine what is "of first importance" for him and this community. Followers of Judaism determine differently.

It was his Damascus experience and some careful theologizing—under the tutelage of Peter (*Gal* 1.18) and in missionary labor—that brought Paul to the point of being able to sketch out for the Corinthians in equally carefully crafted language a valid credal formula centering on the Paschal Mystery of Jesus. The evangelists who reflected the same creed in the structure of their different but similar Gospels achieved such unanimity not in isolation but within a believing—and theologizing—community. It was only when theologians lost that integrating contact with the whole community that their theology became unbalanced—like the rival schools of Alexandria and Antioch feuding over one approach to Jesus rather than another, like Augustine deprived of the healthier attitude to humanity and healing of the Greek Fathers, like the West as a whole lacking living contact with the East for so long.

THEOLOGIZING IN COMMUNITY

Theology—healthy theology—is thus a community, ecclesial, "churchy" endeavor, as valid faith is ecclesial. The divine offer of life—*koinonia* in the language of the New Testament—comes within a saved and saving community. It is responded to most adequately by participating in that community and benefiting from its tradition of the experience of the foundational band of disciples. That tradition is manifold; we have seen the unnecessary agony and peril of those who choose to tap into a single form of tradition (like the biblical), which may at times come under close scrutiny or undergo necessary reform. Church, a community of life, does offer its members a variety of ways to participate in that life. Its theologians can take as their source biblical and liturgical traditions, doctrinal and indeed theological traditions; for each religious community—Jewish, Christian and others—develops its own distinctive framework, concepts and idioms of theologizing.

So in making sense of our Christian faith by normal theological processes, we are at an advantage by living within the community of the Christian Church (other faith traditions could speak similarly). We are also rendering that community a service in helping them all bring understanding to faith. And yet at times theologians can feel uncomfortable within the Church, and at times the Church can seem to resent the presence and activity of those rendering this service. For this the theologians may be at fault, perhaps by misunderstanding their role or by playing it in the halfhearted fashion to which theologians have always been tempted with a view to appeasement:

For they are a rebellious people,
    faithless children,
children who will not hear
    the instruction of the Lord;
who say to seers, "Do not see;"
    and to prophets, "Do not prophesy to us what is right;
speak to us smooth things, prophesy illusions" (Is 30.9–10).

THEOLOGY'S ROLE IN THE COMMUNITY

On the other hand, the discomfiture of theologians within the Church can come from the community, who themselves mistake the meaning of Church. We noted at times throughout earlier chapters devoted to different periods of the community's theologizing that Church was seen differently—a persecuted "little flock," the powerful favorite of emperors, the exclusive haven of salvation, a congregation of individual readers of the Word. Theology can be asked to provide different services in different models of Church: defending the community's right to exist, championing the status quo, keeping silent before individual interpretation, critiquing decadent forms of tradition, vindicating positions arrived at in defiance of sounder theology—or, as in Isaiah's Jerusalem, speaking smooth things.

For the Church, fundamentally, is a mystery, the divine plan to offer life to all. Paul called it "the mystery of Christ," and felt called to preach to Gentiles the ecclesial dimension of a plan which has cosmic, personal, historical, biblical dimensions as well—truly *polypoikilos*, "multidimensioned" (*Eph* 3.10). It offers its beneficiaries the gift of life through a divine process of sharing, fellowship, *koinonia*: a share in the Gospel (*Phil* 1.5), a share in faith (*Phlm* 6), a share in the Father's life with the Son (*1 Cor* 1.9), a share in the Spirit (*2 Cor* 13.13; *Phil* 2.11) as well as the share we give of our life and goods to others (*2 Cor* 8.1–9).

Yet that community of life can present itself in various ways, under a range of figures and images and models (the New Testament itself offering close on a hundred such images). Theology makes its contribution with varying of success and degrees of ease in one model of Church rather than another—that is, one major way in which the *polypoikilos* community functions, such as that Protestant model of

99

listener and herald of the Word. Stress on the community dimension, with members sharing what they have to offer to one another and with less stress on status and structure, should see theologians encouraged to contribute their work to the development of faith's understanding. The Church may function as pilgrim in the world, moving toward its heavenly goal. It may, like Jesus before it, be a servant of the poor and oppressed. It may function as sign and sacrament of the Father's offer of life. In all these models theology's role is given more or less scope.

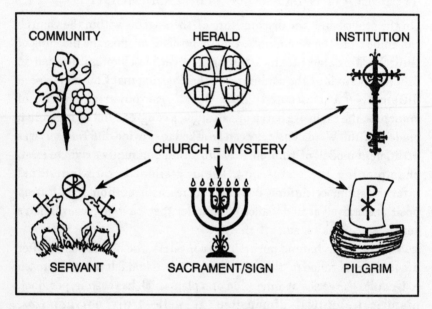

COMMUNITY HERALD INSTITUTION

CHURCH = MYSTERY

SERVANT SACRAMENT/SIGN PILGRIM

Models of Church

MODELS OF COMMUNITY

The various Christian churches reveal at work different models—perhaps several at once. In 1948 a great number of member churches gathered for an initial assembly of the World Council of Churches, defining itself as "a fellowship of churches which confess the Lord Jesus Christ as God and Savior according to the Scriptures." Protestant members would like to be seen as reflecting a herald role, while also often conspicuously discharging a servant role as well, yet perhaps not reflecting a notably sacramental character. The Roman Catholic community, for long not as conspicuous for its attention to the scriptural Word as to liturgical celebration, appears less as herald than as sacramental communion. It also has a strongly institutional character, so that since Counter-Reformation times until this century it could rest easy with Robert Bellarmine's 1586 definition stressing order and identity and authority:

> *The one and true Church is the community of men*
> *brought together by the profession of the same Christian*
> *faith*
> *and conjoined in the communion of the same sacraments,*
> *under the government of the legitimate pastors*
> *and especially the one vicar of Christ on earth, the Roman*
> *pontiff.*

The need of theologians is not clearly specified in such a hierarchized church. It was centuries before their work could bear fruit in bringing this community to a self-understanding (indebted to further biblical study) as Body of Christ, People of God, Light of the Nations (which it achieved at the Second Vatican Council) and more recently in terms of *communio, koinonia*, fellowship, sharing, participation. This latter has also proved fruitful as a basis for ecumenical theologizing in company with Anglicans (in meetings of the Anglican-Roman Catholic International Commission—ARCIC), Orthodox and other churches. ARCIC I admitted this in its *Final Report* in 1982:

> *Fundamental to all our Statements is the concept of*
> koinonia *(communion). In the early Christian tradition,*
> *reflection on the experience of* koinonia *opened the way to*
> *the understanding of the mystery of the Church. Although*
> koinonia *is never equated with "Church" in the New*
> *Testament, it is the term that most aptly expresses the*
> *mystery underlying the various New Testament images of*
> *the Church.*

In 1991 ARCIC II published a complete Statement on *Church as Communion*. The Synod of Bishops in Rome in 1985 had also endorsed this understanding of Church—though the Congregation for the Doctrine of the Faith expressed considerable reservations about ARCIC proceeding down that path.

THEOLOGY, MAGISTERIUM, DISSENT

So theologians and institutional Church do not always achieve a meeting of minds. In the Roman institution authority is centralized, and the community's teaching role, *magisterium*, likewise tends to be, at least at different times. The term "magisterium" in the sense now understood dates in fact only from the nineteenth century. In the early Church we find the happy situation where the bishops were theologians and many of the theologians bishops—though not all. Some great theologians later nominated "Doctors of the Church" were not bishops, like Jerome and (a nominee in our time) Teresa of Avila! At medieval councils a vote was given on doctrinal matters to theologians on the grounds that they enjoyed an authority that "greatly exceeds that of an individual bishop or an ignorant abbot or titular," as was agreed at the Council of Constance in 1415. But after Trent, in the defensive Counter-Reformation climate, doctrinal competence came to be assumed under hierarchical, juridical authority.

While a Bellarmine-style ecclesiology is in force, theological competence can be divorced from hierarchical jurisdiction. The ideal, on the contrary, is that official teaching, magisterium, encourages the unity of the community's faith by promoting a truth highlighted by scholarly endeavor and reflection, as in the patristic model. Where this compenetration of theology and community teaching does not occur, legitimate *dissent* can arise from scholars anxious to retain integrity but can be dismissed as disloyalty. It is to their bishops, however, that the community looks for an authentic expression of ecclesial faith, not a theologian advancing personal views that have yet to mature; "dissent" is improperly applied to such theological positions.

The fine relationship between theology and magisterium is not always patent to members of other communities, even when well balanced. When the balance is lost, the Catholic Church is seen as authoritarian and foreign to Käsemann's "hearing and obeying community" responding to the Word. Protestant and Orthodox communities find uninviting and alarmingly non-biblical a Church where theological exploration becomes superfluous, disloyal even; mystery of Christ and sharing of life seem to have succumbed to an authoritarian institution. They have sympathy with Catholic theologians who choose to explore not smooth things but the rough and the hard things of faith and morals in a rapidly developing world and find themselves called to account to doctrinal authority, especially if the media give prominence to their work.

Far preferable is an ecclesiology of which John Paul II often speaks in his letter following the 1987 Synod on the laity:

> *Vatican Council II has invited us to contemplate the mystery of the Church through biblical images which bring to light the reality of the Church as a* communion *with its inseparable dimensions: the communion of each Christian with Christ and the communion of all Christians with one another. There is the sheep-fold, the flock, the vine, the spiritual building, the Holy City . . .*
> The reality of the Church as Communion is, *then, the integrating aspect, indeed* the central content of the "mystery," *or rather, the divine plan for the salvation of humanity* (emphasis original).

Both John and Paul would concur with John Paul in this understanding of Church. So too would the Fathers, not just Clement and Origen in Alexandria, who gave no pride of place to bishops in communicating the apostolic tradition, but Irenaeus, who urged popes to look for consensus rather than excommunication where there is disagreement. Aquinas, too, did not confine doctrinal magisterium to bishops alone. Making sense of faith, theology's task, is surely the task of the whole community; proceeding to definition—the end of the process but also the beginning, in Rahner's words—is a different responsibility.

SOME FURTHER READING

Theology's role in the community and the treatment theologians receive depend, as we have seen in several chapters, on the community's own understanding of itself as Church. Isaiah's "rebellious people," Käsemann's Reformation model of hearing and obeying community, Bellarmine's corporation model, the World Council of Churches speaking of a fellowship of communities, Orthodox accent on mystery, ARCIC presenting Church in terms of *koinonia*, John Paul II writing in *Christifideles Laici* of vine and branches—all will allow theologians a different role and expect from them a different contribution, from compliant development of formulated doctrine to active exploration of the implications of tradition in all its forms. Ecclesiology has undergone considerable development in recent decades in all Christian groups— Anglican, Catholic, Orthodox, Protestant. The Catholic community's growing understanding from Pope Pius XII's *Mystici Corporis Christi* in 1943 through Vatican II and recent synods, along with contemporary theological elaboration, I have outlined in *Mystery of Life. A Theology of Church*, Melbourne: CollinsDove, 1990.

The turnaround in Catholic ecclesiology derived in large part from Pius XII's promotion of biblical studies in the community, enabling Church to be seen in terms of biblical figures and images and thus to escape the constraints of a Counter-Reformation institutional model. In his *Images of the Church in the New Testament*, Philadelphia: Westminster, 1960, Paul Minear listed close on a hundred such biblical figures. Capitalizing on the development of scientific models, theologians began to speak of models of Church, as Avery Dulles does in a book of that name (Garden City: Doubleday, 1974). For Dulles, images "employed reflectively and critically to develop one's theoretical understanding of a reality" are models. He lists such models as institution, mystical communion, sacrament, herald, servant. We have seen theologians feeling more or less at ease in one or other model of Church. Karl Rahner, in a key address, published as "Towards a fundamental theological intepretation of Vatican II," *Theological Studies* 40 (1979), 716–27, sees the effect of the Council as establishing a world Church, a development equal in significance to the change from a Church of the Jews to a Church of the Gentiles in Paul's time. He doubts if a heavy-handed Roman centralism can do justice to this.

Dulles has also written on the developing understanding of "magisterium." He notes the late appearance of an exclusively hierarchical, juridical notion of magisterium, which he sees as betraying the patristic notion of "consensus" that is still alive in Orthodox theology and has recently been revived in World Council circles. In an essay, "The magisterium in history: theological considerations" in his *A Church to Believe in*, New York: Crossroad, 1992, he regrets the development:

From the standpoint of the theology of magisterium, the post-Tridentine period represents the triumph of juridicism. The many instances of teaching authority recognized in the New Testament and in earlier church history are in effect reduced to one—the hierarchical, which is itself progressively reduced to the single voice of the papacy. The teaching activity of the papacy is reduced to its juridical headship (112–13).

This same development is reinforced in the Roman *Instruction on the Ecclesial Role of the Theologian* from the Congregation for the Doctrine of the Faith in 1990. The passive role of the theologian as explicating defined doctrine, proposed in Pius IX's *Inter gravissimas* and Pius XII's *Humani Generis*, is restated, and dissent (the apparent focus of the Instruction) disallowed. As we suggested often, such a role is encouraged within a theology of Church which has not kept pace with other magisterial statements, such as Vatican II.

Ladislas Orsy in *The Church: Learning and Teaching. Magisterium, Assent, Dissent, Academic Freedom*, Wilmington: Michael Glazier, 1987, discusses whether Dulles can rightly speak of a dual magisterium in the Church, exercised respectively by hierarchy and by theologians—something the 1990 Instruction would veto. He thinks such usage, justified in history or not, would be confusing, though conceding "the church has not failed in according solemn recognition (rarely adverted to) to this non-hierarchical teaching power," having in mind Doctors of the Church who are not bishops. Jerome and Bede—and Teresa—can rest content, as can the community who have benefited from their theologizing.

EXERCISES IN THEOLOGY

1. Do you have a clear sense of living in a community of faith? What supports does that experience bring to you? Or do you feel on your own in your journey of faith?
2. Is it a difficult task to be a prophet in today's Church? Can you think of theologians or others who are prophetic? How does the community respond to them?
3. What do you see as the limits to the role of the theologian in the Church? How does a bishop's role differ from a theologian's? Do you know bishops who are good theologians? Should every bishop be one?

11

Theology and morality

An alternative title to this chapter might have been "Making sense of morals." In that case an opening paragraph would need to be directed to demonstrating that theology has something to do with morality as well as faith and that Anselm had just overlooked this in his definition of theology. "Faith and morals" is an unfortunately disjunctive phrase, implying some sort of division between faith and life, between what we believe and how we live. Aquinas has been both help and hindrance in this regard. We noted his incorporation of the Christian life in the *Secunda Pars* of the *Summa Theologiae*, yet his intellectualist definition of faith long stood in need of correction: "the act of the intellect assenting to divine truth under the dominion of the will as moved by God's grace." A "north of the eyebrows" statement of faith, as a friend of mine would say.

"FAITH AND MORALS"?

In Chapter 1 we saw Vatican II correcting Aquinas's limited definition and Vatican I's adoption of it, by insisting that faith involves also the commitment of the whole person to God. And multitudes of good people daily demonstrate their faith in their lives of virtue and even heroism; we cited Mother Teresa and her work for the destitute. The Old Testament knew the corrective had to be applied, if faith meant "saying Amen to God." All our lives, our whole being, not just "north of the eyebrows," must be involved in a faith response to a divine self-communication that is equally wholly personal.

To an extent, however, biblical scholarship has contributed to the compartmentalizing of faith and morals. Under the influence of the great German Lutheran tradition-historians like Gerhard Von Rad, attention in Old Testament study focused on Torah and Prophets as constituting the *magnalia Dei*, God's great interventions in Israel's salvation history. The third part of TaNaK, *Ketubim*, The Writings, were neglected as being less historically oriented. In the former, moral principles arise from those spectacular divine epiphanies on Mount Sinai (or Horeb) which we read in association with Decalogue and Book of the Covenant and prophetic recall to these in the course of Conquest and national defense. Even "ethnic cleansing" could thus claim direct divine command, or positive law, as could minuscule details of Jewish life, such as dietary matters.

The morality of The Writings, especially that great body of moral teaching that is Wisdom (in *Proverbs, Job, Ecclesiastes, Sirach, Wisdom of Solomon* and parts of other books), could not claim and does not invoke such a spectacular and respectable font. It is simply content to express what people have found by sheer *experience* to be true of the way the world is. It is a pragmatic, empirical, sometimes banal morality, deriving its principles from the real world and contesting the faulty formulation of these on the lips of inexpert, overly religious traditionalists, like the friends Job scornfully puts to right about the likelihood of our all getting our just deserts here and now:

> *No doubt you are the people,*
> * and wisdom will die with you*
> *But I have understanding as well as you;*
> * I am not inferior to you.*
> *The tents of robbers are at peace,*
> * and those who provoke God are secure* (12.2–3,6).

No need to invoke the God of Sinai and tablets of stone; just face the facts, says Job, and drop the pious claptrap.

THE NORM OF REASON AND EXPERIENCE

Job would be amused to think he is invoking no more and no less than what later moralists would style the eternal law, "the way things are," and our participation in it through reason, natural law. He (that is, the sage who is his author) is a believer but does not parade his religious beliefs unnecessarily. His God—not the God of Sinai nor of the patriarchs—is the provident God of the observable cosmos who creates and conducts it with a Wisdom (the eternal law) that surpasses human wisdom. Job thus does not need to cite divine positive law. The sages, unlike the prophets, rarely do, though their appreciation of natural law is in constant process of refinement (as is ours)—as Job tells his friends.

That refinement, within the covers of the Old Testament, for one thing does not reach to a proper appreciation of the status of women. Qoheleth, the authors of *Proverbs* and Ben Sira have some demeaning things to say about them (plus some strangely noble sentiments about Woman Wisdom, too). With this exception, we can recognize in the morality of the sages a realism and dependence on reason and experience that Aquinas would find appealing in Aristotle's moral stance.

The moral dimension of New Testament theology, too, takes this twofold accent. God has spoken again in Jesus, the New Moses on a new mountain giving a New Torah. The Old Law, the Old Covenant, the old relationship is sustained and transformed in the person, life, ministry and eminently in the Paschal Mystery of Jesus. Paul, who spends much of his missionary activity refuting claims of Judaizers in most communities that all Gentile converts must conform to Mosaic Law and therefore is often misrepresented as being anti-law, in fact tells the Galatians they must fulfill the Law of Christ (6.2). So morality becomes incorporated in Jesus, especially the Jesus of the Beatitudes and sermons and parables. But in the New Testament there are the sages, too, who invoke the broader principles and norms of reason and popular experience in addition to the positive law of the Mount. Jesus himself is among them, eminently a sage—"a greater than Solomon is here"— referring his listeners to "the way things are," the eternal law of a provident God who sends his blessings and makes his demands on all alike. James is a sage, too, so pedestrian in his morality and heedless of Gospel-style positive law as later to earn Luther's scorn—yet again we catch the echo of Job and Aristotle both.

There is thus a balance in biblical morality—if looked at in its totality. The balance has not always been respected. *Religion* will tend to focus on the revealed pronouncements of divine positive law, from the God of Sinai or the Jesus of the Mount of the Beatitudes, without perhaps attending to the considerable conditioning that these pronouncements have undergone (compare the differing sets of Decalogues and Beatitudes our texts offer us). *Theology* should advert to these contextual elements in biblical texts, but as we have seen it has not always been able to resist the attraction of spectacular epiphanies in favor of the more mundane moralizing (as with Von Rad and Luther). Sound moral theology—in any religious tradition—will need to focus on values underlying norms no matter how spectacularly given, on the human being as the maker of moral decisions, on the real world as the context of our moral lives. To do less than that is to demean the creator God, as Job well knew.

BALANCE IN MORAL THEOLOGY

Christian moral tradition, predictably, is a story of oscillation between one principle and another—between the divine and the human in morality, between the legal and the personal, between the revealed and the rational, between moral pessimism and optimism. We have noted often the differences between East and West in terms of moral attitudes. Irenaeus, expatriate easterner in the West in the late second century, retains his native optimism and accent on the personal in proposing Jesus as the model of the human being living life to the full and developing all one's potential:

> *The Word makes God visible to human beings in his*
> *countless mysteries lest they, totally deprived of the vision*
> *of God, lose hold of his very existence. For the glory of God*
> *is the human being fully alive, and the life of the human*
> *being is the vision of God* (Adversus Haereses IV,7).

It is an uplifting and encouraging ideal. In Africa, Augustine, with his manichean background and his own checkered career, could not take so rosy a view of human potential. Rather, human depravity and the sin inherited from our forebears. In fact, it is to Augustine's literalist interpretation of the story of the Fall in *Genesis* 3 that the Council of Trent's definition of original sin is to be traced. While the East does not deny the reality of sin, it forsakes the Western imagery of criminal and judge for the notion of disease and healing. Gabriel Daly recommends that we take the Eastern approach:
"It is the process of healing which is primarily revealed: we know of the disease partly from human experience but mainly, and salvifically, from what Jesus Christ has done for us by his life, teaching, death and resurrection."

Not that the East is free of all imbalance. Chrysostom, attracting modern criticism for some anti-Semitism, seems more conspicuous for inheriting that misogynism which we found typical of Old Testament

Wisdom. When he deals with the Fall in his *Genesis* commentary, we are struck by the fact that for him it has little dogmatic significance but proves rather an occasion for moralizing, in the course of which the arch-criminal is not Adam but Eve:

> *Why did you make your husband a partner in this grievous disaster, why prove to be the temptress of the person whose helpmate you were intended to be, and why for a tiny morsel alienate him along with yourself from the favor of God? What excess of folly led you to such heights of presumption? Wasn't it sufficient for you to pass your life without care or concern, clad in a body yet free of any bodily needs? to enjoy everything in the garden except for one tree? to have all visible things under your own authority and to exercise control over them all? Did you instead, deceived as you were by vain hopes, set your heart on reaching the very pinnacle of power?*

Over the years Christian moralists will find a like eloquence in elaborating on the weaknesses of women.

The element of balance that Aquinas—but not all the medieval systematizers—brought to moral theology was his synthesis of two approaches, the biblical with its accent on divine positive law, and the Aristotelian with its emphasis on reason and experience (as found also in that other biblical strand, Wisdom). For Aquinas ethics, the development of moral principles, is an empirical science; it depends on our knowledge, and is therefore subject to change (we, not he, have come to accept the principle of religious liberty, for example). He would not agree with his commentators' accent on moral acts independent of the acting person in all morally relevant circumstances—a caricature that came to be accepted as the classical approach in the Catholic community. He would not agree with the "Voluntarism" of his contemporary systematizer John Duns Scotus and Augustine before him, so anxious to uphold the divine will (Latin *voluntas*) as to undermine the role of reason. On the other hand, we would not agree with his lack of contact with basic Christian experiences, such as the relegation of Jesus' Paschal Mystery we noted in Chapter 7 in considering the design of the *Summa*. Hence Luther's remark, "In the Scholastics I lost Christ."

111

RECOVERING A BIBLICAL DIMENSION

So medieval moral theology could lose its balance. It also failed to balance the legal and the personal in approaching human behavior in the sacrament of reconciliation. The development of manuals for confessors dealt rather with categories of sins and appropriate penalties than with the biblical notion of reconciliation on the model of the parables of *Luke* 15. Advances in biblical criticism following the Renaissance, therefore, promised to renew moral theology and sacramental practice. A more sophisticated grasp of authorship and composition of sacred texts took account of development and cultural conditioning. Those fundamental texts, Decalogue and Sermon on the Mount, could be seen less as verbatim reports of divine intervention than as later reworked versions bearing the imprint of contemporary concerns, and thus necessarily lacking uniformity. A more comprehensive biblical theology revealed the whole covenantal framework of the Decalogue, so that the item missing from Christian catechesis, "I am the Lord your God, *who brought you out of the land of Egypt, out of the house of bondage*" (*Ex* 20.2), could be seen as vital to a morality that was not to be simply arbitrary but a response to divine initiative. Thus the Decalogue could take its place as the opening items of a treaty form relating two powers of the contemporary orient, and so serve in the Bible as a figure of the closely personal relationship between Yahweh and Israel, between God and each human person. The centrality of the Paschal Mystery in New Testament thought was restored, to refocus Christian theology and liturgy both. Wisdom material in both testaments returned to favor, with its acceptance of the rational, the experiential, the circumstantial in moral decision making.

In our time, therefore, being able to enjoy an overview of various developments in moral theologizing Eastern and Western, and also the further light that biblical criticism sheds on the true significance of inspired texts, we should be able to achieve the requisite balance. Different trends still appear, however. Protestant theology, under the influence of Reformers like John Calvin and moderns like Karl Barth, is still anxious to preserve the sovereignty of God and the personal nature of his dealings and commands—what we have called Voluntarism, a kind of moral fundamentalism. That can be seen also in some Catholic statements (as can biblical fundamentalism), which take an increasingly positivistic and authoritarian tone, in contrast to Vatican II's emphasis on the human basis of morality and encouragement of personal decision making on the myriad new challenges facing us:

> *The People of God believes that it is led by the Spirit of the Lord, who fills the earth. Motivated by this faith, it labors to decipher authentic signs of God's presence and purpose in the happenings, needs, and desires in which this People has a part along with other people of our age. For faith throws a new light on everything, manifests God's design for our total vocation, and thus directs the mind to solutions which are fully human* (Gaudium et Spes 11*)*.

MORALITY HUMAN AND CHRISTIAN

The number and range of moral problems facing humanity that call for response are immense; the task of a sound moral theology is urgent. We have lived through world wars and still experience fierce national conflicts. Questions about life and health, abortion and AIDS, euthanasia and IVF face moralists and medical practitioners daily. Global survival and distribution of resources, conservation and Third World debt cannot be kept off the moral agenda. People today look for guidance, and yet cherish moral independence. Pope Paul VI's encyclical *Humanae Vitae* on the regulation of birth, following a painstaking process instigated by John XIII in 1963 in the wake of statements on the question by Pius XI and Pius XII, was received by the world in a manner that could at best be called ambiguous. A rather better response greeted John Paul II's *Veritatis Splendor* in 1993, but acceptance was hardly universal. This very lengthy encyclical could claim:

> *This is the first time, in fact, that the Magisterium of the Church has set forth the fundamental elements of this teaching, and presented the principles for the pastoral discernment necessary in practical and cultural situations which are complex and even crucial* (115*)*.

The moral issues such statements by Christian teaching bodies arouse, however, go beyond rulings on individual matters, such as the lawfulness of artificial contraception. There is a basic consideration: to whom is the statement addressed? Do the moral principles invoked speak to all people, or only to members of one (relatively small) religious community? Should the principles and norms be more universally applicable? Does the teaching authority unnecessarily forfeit appeal to such human, universal moral principles, and instead cite sources peculiar to the one community (like the Bible, or the Catholic magisterium)? Is there an implication that there are no universally valid moral values and principles and norms? Or would the teaching not stand up against them? Is morality thought by the composer to be basically Christian, basically religious, or basically human? Further, what are the bounds of the community within which the statement is thought relevant and applicable? What theology of Church underlies the statement?

These are relevant theological issues to raise in connection with any religious community's moral teaching. It is interesting that Neuner and Dupuis, who have collected magisterial statements on the Christian life over the ages by the Catholic community in their *The Christian Faith*, make this observation:

"As to the specifically Christian principles of human conduct, they are poorly represented in official documents, which deal with Christian morality in a general way. Intimately connected as these principles are with life itself, they have often been taken for granted rather than explicitly stated by the Church's teaching office."

That is a hoped-for conclusion, considering the positive developments over the centuries since biblical times that we have reviewed above. A balance, albeit delicate, was being achieved on moral issues that avoided the extremes of utter rationalism, on the one hand, and voluntarism, biblicism and authoritarianism, on the other. It would be a pity if the magisterium did not reflect such balance. It could also be that at present the balance is at risk, as it has been at times in the past in one community or another.

SOME FURTHER READING

It is said a good teacher of moral theology is a *rara avis*. That is probably a reflection on the difficulty of achieving the balance of which this chapter has spoken. My own experience included a moral professor who confined himself to recounting case histories, scornfully rejecting requests for guidance at the level of principle with the remark, "Oh, you can get that in any old textbook." Be that as it may (not all texts in fact achieve balance), a good account of the development of moral theology in the Catholic community, distinguishing the truly Thomistic empiricism from what later came to be known as the "classical" approach, can be found in Arnold Hogan's *On Being Catholic Today. What Kind of Person Should I Be?*, Melbourne: CollinsDove, 1993. This book also enjoys the advantage of a knowledge of moral theory in other Christian communities and input from a Protestant moralist.

The question of the specifically Christian character of morality is much discussed; it has obvious implications for moral education. We noted the fact that Catholic official teaching has tended to accentuate the human basis to morality and presume attention to the religious; *Veritatis Splendor* may be an exception. For a thorough examination of this key issue see Brian Lewis, "What is distinctive about Christian ethics?", *Word in Life* 42 (1993 No.3), 5–10.

The doctrine of original sin was given above as an example of the different moral approaches of West and East. The term does not, in fact, rate a mention in the East in the first millennium—as it is also interesting that the *Genesis* account of the Fall never occurs again in the Old Testament in prophet, psalmist or historian. Neil Ormerod in *Grace and Disgrace* traces the Western development of the doctrine from Augustine's (personally conditioned) and Aquinas's literalist reading of that biblical text through the Reformation to the Council of Trent. This helpful account gains much from an appendix by John Chryssavgis, "Original sin—an Orthodox perspective." We clearly have a case here of the rethinking of a doctrine in the light of better knowledge of the whole of Christian tradition and advances in biblical criticism— just as we now appreciate better the Decalogue (and divine positive law generally), something which emerges from a work like Eduard Nielsen's *The Ten Commandments in New Perspective* (1965), Eng. trans., London: SCM, 1968.

On medico-moral questions the Catholic magisterium has made statements in the wake of *Humanae Vitae*. The Congregation for the Doctrine of the Faith published in 1975 a *Declaration on Certain Questions concerning Sexual Ethics* reaffirming the teaching of the encyclical on the regulation of birth as well as traditional teaching on premarital sexual intercourse, homosexuality and masturbation. In 1987 the same congregation's *Instruction on Respect for Human Life in its Origin and on the Dignity of Procreation* disallowed *in vitro* fertilization and embryo transfer techniques. In 1995 John Paul II's *Evangelium Vitae* gave further accent to a "culture of life." On social questions there has been a long series of encyclical-style statements, from Leo XIII's *Rerum Novarum* in 1891 to John Paul II's *Laborem Exercens* a century later. Likewise, on the moral implications of development and under-development the popes have spoken: John XXIII in *Pacem in Terris* in 1963, Paul VI's *Progressio Populorum* in 1967 and John Paul II's *Sollicitudo Rei Socialis* in 1987.

EXERCISES IN THEOLOGY

1. Do you find that in moral decision making your first port of call is biblical versions of divine statements? Is the basis of your morality thus *religious*? Or are you ready to recognize first the moral implications of being *human*?

2. Look at the 1993 encyclical *Veritatis Splendor*, and in particular its structure based on three chapters. Do you find that it moves logically from human to religious and then to Christian and specifically Catholic morality? Or does its order of treatment imply that only Catholics can benefit from the principles laid out?

3. What are the implications of a balanced moral theology for moral education? In your experience, are parents/teachers too insistent on norms and laws rather than values? And where is it best to look for these values if one wants to appeal to the young: in the words of the Decalogue or from the mouth of Jesus? In legal sanctions? In human nature and experience ("the way things are")?

12

Theology and theologies

We made the obvious point in Chapter 1 that theology is not all words and writing, even if it is expressed at all. Believers have endeavored over the ages to make sense of what they believe through a range of media—music, drama, film, sculpture, dance and mime, the graphic and plastic arts. The faithful have been led to an understanding of the faith by the talents of all these artists—and, of course, by their individual theologies. For what one artist finds merely pathetic in one of the mysteries of Jesus' life, for instance, another may represent as excruciating; their different theologies lie at the basis of these representations. Consider, for example, how differently East and West greet the Easter event—with the full-throated jubilation of Handel's Alleluia chorus, and the slow solemn reverence of Rimsky-Korsakov's "The Great Russian Easter."

HOW TO INTERPRET THE MYSTERIES

I have always found helpful in accepting this fact the volume published by the World Council of Churches in Geneva for Hans-Ruedi Weber, *On a Friday Noon. Meditations under the Cross*, a collection of thirty-three prints of the Crucifixion from various periods and countries. One of the Old Masters, that by Diego Velazquez in seventeenth-century Spain, we all recognize. It shows the dead Jesus, a beautifully proportioned figure somewhat marked by blood in places but apparently in repose as it stands almost comfortably on the cross. To turn to a later plate, "The Tortured Christ" by Brazilian Guido Rocha, is to be shocked out of this gentle sorrow. It is a fearsome, skeletal, screaming criminal, carved in gleaming metal, mouth wide open in protest and agony, knees drawn right up to protrude directly in front. No comfortable pathos here. Weber comments:

"Rocha does not think of Jesus as the Son of God, the sacrifice offered for our sins or in any other such classic Christian dogmatic ways . . . Here was a man who passed through the deepest sufferings and nevertheless remained fully human."

Both Velazquez and Rocha believe, and for them the Crucifixion is a basic article of faith. But they have theologized differently about their faith in a dying Jesus, as have other artists in the thought-provoking collection. Their medium conveys their theology powerfully, if not equally so. There is more to it than artistry, however. We might observe that seventeenth-century Spain, which certainly knew death and suffering, could not condone as food for meditation by the faithful in respectable churches an obscene figure like Rocha's; ours hardly can. As well, gifted artists like Velazquez did not feel called, like Rocha, to bring commentary on social conditions into religious subjects. Weber says of the several South American reproductions, "For many Latin American Christians the righteous are those who suffer from oppression and struggle for justice. Therefore Jesus on the cross is very near to them." For Velazquez, the expression of faith did not require this dimension, or perhaps he had never experienced a like desolation.

So we bring to the task of theology all we are and have—our upbringing and formation, heredity even, our social and religious background, in fact our whole cultural setting. In my own family there are those whose theology I cannot share entirely, though we were raised on a similar Irish-style Catholicism. A senior relative of mine recently chose in his declining years to outlay much of his modest resources to travel to another hemisphere to visit the shrine of Our Lady at Garabandal. I felt inclined, but would never have been rash enough, to say to him, "Uncle, before going to such trouble to visit the site of a possible Marian appearance, why not first have the certainty of meeting the Word of God in all the pages of the Bible"—which I am sure he had never done. My theology found contradiction in what he was going to much trouble to achieve; his theology suggested otherwise to him.

THEOLOGY AND CULTURE

I may theologize differently from my Orthodox and Protestant friends on account of my Catholic formation, reading and practice. Like them I believe in "one Lord, one faith, one baptism, one God and Father of all" (*Eph* 4.5–6). But unlike the former I am content to have the *filioque* clause about the procession of the Spirit appear in any creed I recite (though less presumptuously than occurred with its insertion by Rome into the Nicene-Constantinopolitan Creed in the sixth century). And unlike many of the latter my theologizing would take account of liturgical and doctrinal traditions of our and my community. Amongst my Catholic friends I would find those whose theology differs from mine, for similar reasons. Their model of Church would not be mine; I am no longer happy with Bellarmine's institutional model, though I was certainly brought up to it and though I admit a necessary institutional, incarnational component to Church, as I do to Jesus.

Within my church, also, I feel free to choose one theology rather than another even about major matters of faith, like divine revelation and the person of Jesus. To me the former appears in its true context and with all the notes of gratuity, personal character and communicability when presented, as Vatican II's Constitution on Revelation does (*DV* 1), in the light of John's statement of the divine communication of life:

> *This life was revealed, and we have seen it and testify to it, and declare to you the eternal life that was with the Father and was revealed to us. We declare to you what we have seen and heard so that you also may have fellowship with us; and truly our fellowship is with the Father and with his Son Jesus Christ* (1 Jn 1.2–3).

This accent on fellowship, sharing, *koinonia*, life, does greater justice to divine revelation, in my view, than the model of the unwrapped package which we saw to be implied in Paul's catechetical process about the Paschal Mystery in *1 Cor* 15.1–5, with its primary accent on fidelity of transmission. Such a model also seems to underly the Pope's introduction of the new *Catechism* in the apostolic constitution, entitled significantly and no doubt programmatically *Fidei Depositum*, "the deposit of faith," again with the accent on fidelity rather than (but not exclusive of) vitality.

A RANGE OF THEOLOGIES

My community also offers me, in its Scriptures, its liturgy, its doctrine, its piety, a range of theologies of Jesus. Many of these have been explored and depicted in Christian art: the babe of Bethlehem, the juvenile

119

dispenser of wisdom in the Temple, the carpenter of Nazareth, the itinerant preacher, the transfigured Lord, the Ecce Homo, the crucified victim of Velazquez and Rocha. In 1984 the Pontifical Biblical Commission offered its readers a wide range of recognized approaches to Jesus.

Some contemporary approaches to Jesus

1. The Jesus of Councils and Creeds: classical Christology
2. Modern speculative approach
3. Scientific historical approach to the historical Jesus
4. Approach of the comparative study of religions school
5. Approach from the study of Judaism
6. Approach from salvation history, emphasizing titles of Jesus
7. Anthropological approach
8. Existentialist , demythologizing approach, using form criticism
9. Approach of liberation theologians and social scientists
10. Approach of a new systematic theology
11. Christologies "from above" and "from below"

My devotion and my theology may move from one such approach to another. My uncle at Garabandal may not have found any of them helpful, yet his attachment to Jesus in faith as a daily communicant was beyond question.

"The Bible Alone," we saw in Chapter 9, is one approach to Christian theology resting on one source; its perils we outlined together with the advantage of being able to tap into other forms of tradition of the foundational Christian experience. Yet even a more rounded theology is susceptible of many variations depending on the approach adopted to these traditional forms, such as the doctrinal; magisterial statements can be read in a fundamentalist way, without discrimination, or alternatively read according to the conditions of their formulation (as *Mysterium Ecclesiae* recommended, we saw), probably depending on one's theology of Church. Likewise, in theological formation liturgy can be relegated to a mere study of rubrics, or can be recognized, in the manner of Cyril of Jerusalem and Ambrose, as *theologia prima*, the primary locus and source of theology, as some of today's liturgists would like. As to approaches and methods in scriptural exegesis and interpretation, they are manifold and have implications for all fields of theology, beyond Christology. Following its 1984 statement, the Pontifical Biblical Commission released in 1993 an Instruction on *The Interpretation of the Bible in the Church*, listing the range of methods and approaches developed since the historical-critical method of previous centuries, any of which is preferable for good theologizing to a fundamentalist approach.

Methods and approaches to Scripture in theology

Historical-critical method, including
- textual criticism
- linguistic and semantic analysis
- literary criticism
- genre criticism
- tradition criticism
- redaction criticism

New methods of literary analysis:
- rhetorical analysis
- narrative analysis
- semiotic analysis

Approaches based on tradition:
- canonical approach
- Jewish traditions of interpretation
- history of interpretation

Approaches using the human sciences:
- sociological approach
- approach through cultural anthropology
- psychological and psychoanalytical approaches

Contextual approaches:
- liberationist approach
- feminist approach

THEOLOGY IN CONTEXT

As our faith depends on experience—the community's, too, but also our own personal journey—so does our theologizing. The God we speak of in our theology has already spoken to us in our daily life. Of course, we can (try to) bracket that life out, and make the same effort in reading other theologians. We can ignore the different historical situations of Deuteronomist and Chronicler that determined the different theologies they give us of God's action in Israel's history. We can choose to see Paul homing in on personal justification without regard for the larger question facing him since Damascus of the place of both Jew and Gentile within one chosen people. That is somewhat akin to endeavoring to theologize about Jesus without taking account of his Jewishness and maleness and place in a first-century oriental culture. Akin, too, to pondering the Crucifixions of Velazquez and Rocha without taking account of the life situations that produced such different interpretations of the one mystery.

Much contemporary theology, therefore, is contextual in the way the Biblical Commission speaks of biblical interpretation. Theologians living in social and political situations where people are deprived and suffering need to reconcile that with their faith and, if irreconcilable because unjust in its roots, suggest its inadequacies, as Job did. Walter Brueggemann believes that the book of *Job* is in fact a lament about the breakdown of social structures. Latin American theologian Gustavo Gutierrez expressed a similar modern lament in his book *A Theology of Liberation*, thus pioneering a now widespread movement arising out of a method of doing theology.

> *The theology of liberation attempts to reflect on the experience and meaning of the faith based on the commitment to abolish injustice and to build a new society; this theology must be verified by the practice of that commitment, by active, effective participation in the struggle which the exploited classes have undertaken against their oppressors.*

Such a method of making sense of faith is also political, suggesting the need to alter relationships in society if God's values—the *basileia* Jesus

preached so often, and eminently in the Beatitudes—are to be respected.
If we like to think Jesus is not political in this way, we need only read his
program at the beginning of his ministry in *Luke* 4:

> *The Spirit of the Lord is upon me,*
> *because he has anointed me*
> *to bring good news to the poor.*
> *He has sent me to proclaim release to the captives*
> *and recovery of sight to the blind,*
> *to let the oppressed go free,*
> *to proclaim the year of the Lord's favor.*

Women theologians have long sensed that there is a gap between faith
and social and religious structures, even biblical and magisterial
statements, and that the position of women in these structures and
statements is not what faith would suggest. Women exegetes like Phyllis
Trible, Letty Russell, Elizabeth Schüssler Fiorenza and Rosemary
Radford Ruether have brought to our attention the inequities in the
world of the Bible and in the way the Bible mediates that world. Women
readers of books of the Bible, even those that bear a woman's name like
Ruth and *Judith*, easily detect the hand of a man in the composition,
not to mention those extraordinarily insensitive passages that Phyllis
Trible has highlighted in *Texts of Terror*. The biblical bias, in the view
of feminist theologians, has dictated or helped to reinforce social and
ecclesiastical structures that discriminate against women. It has also
encouraged the use in theology of concepts and language about God
that inadequately express the divine–human relationship and impair
our understanding of Jesus. Feminist theology on these issues has
promoted debate about women's position in Church ministry, resulting
in the ordination of women in the Church of England and the papal
response in 1994, the letter *On reserving priestly ordination to men
alone* reasserting the 1977 decision of Paul VI:

> *The real reason is that, in giving the Church her*
> *fundamental constitution, her theological anthropology—*
> *thereafter always followed by the Church's Tradition—*
> *Christ established things this way.*

OTHER THEOLOGICAL METHODS

Theological anthropology, in fact, becomes a feature of other contemporary methods in theology. Instead of beginning with the Bible or magisterial statement, theologians like Karl Rahner and Bernard Lonergan concentrate on the human being. In being indebted less to such traditional sources than to philosophy, in particular that of Emanuel Kant and specifically his process of transcendental deduction, their method is classed also as transcendental. Rahner's philosophical theology begins with the human being as capable of the divine self-communication (demonstrated preeminently in Jesus) and called to self-transcendence.

> *This immediate self-communication of God to spiritual creatures takes place in what we call "grace" while this self-communication is still in its historical process, and "glory" when it reaches fulfillment.*
>
> FOUNDATIONS OF CHRISTIAN FAITH, 190

Because Rahner considers God's intervention in human history, his anthropological, transcendental theology may be called historical, but not in the sense of those contextual theologians who recognize the implications of contemporary history for human beings. Bernard Lonergan is equally philosophical and Kantian in his theologizing, but his focus is the human being as the knowing person. He traces in his epistemo-theological method, outlined in his *Method in Theology*, a series of stages in the process of uncovering and transmitting meanings and values, like research and interpretation of faith statements.

Other contemporary theologians and their methods have variously been described as existential (John Macquarrie, Paul Tillich), socio-phenomenological (Edward Schillebeeckx, Jon Sobrino), experiential and hermeneutical (David Tracy). The beginner in theology need not delve into all these. For one thing, as is immediately obvious, all admit a problem with theological language, while their own terminology is not crystal clear. On the other hand, all claim to begin their theologizing with the scriptural text, though this is not always patent (in Rahner, for instance); Aquinas could claim the *Summa* was but a commentary on the Gospels, yet we would recognize in its pages more philosophy than New Testament. All would claim to be endeavoring to relate their theologizing to human experience, but not all would be as close to contemporary concerns as the contextual theologians. What all illustrate, however, is that making sense of faith, the task of theology, can be approached in more ways than one—just as Paul realized the divine plan itself is *polypoikilos*, of a rich variety. Let us adopt our own approach to this rich and varied plan.

SOME FURTHER READING

Theology in art is a subject for which there are abundant materials available from all periods—at least from the catacombs in the case of Christian graphic art, as our cover suggests. Such paleoChristian art finds a place in Hans-Ruedi Weber's companion volume on the Incarnation, *Immanuel. The Coming of Jesus in Art and the Bible*, also published in Geneva for the World Council of Churches, 1984.

Theological models of Church we looked at in Chapter 10. Avery Dulles, who has written of them, has investigated also various models of revelation in a book of that title (Garden City: Doubleday, 1983). He distinguishes revelation as doctrine, as history, as inner experience, as dialectical presence, as new awareness. The implications of the different models for different styles and methods of theologizing are obvious. Sallie McFague deals with models, too, in *Metaphorical Theology: Models of God in Religious Language*, Philadelphia: Fortress, 1982. Of interest to feminist theologians, she looks at the (male) images of the divine–human relationship found in the Bible.

"The critical criterion is not whether the Bible and the tradition contain such metaphors, but whether they are appropriate ones in which to suggest dimensions of the new divine-human relationship intrinsic to this religious tradition" (166-67).

As to the Pontifical Biblical Commission's statement on the Bible and Christology, Joseph A. Fitzmyer, later a member of the Commission, has digested it in "Christology and the Biblical Commission," *America*, December 22, 1984, 417–20.

Walter Brueggemann's article on *Job*, suggesting that we see the book as social criticism, is entitled "Theodicy in a social dimension," *Journal for the Study of the Old Testament* 33 (1985), 3–25. Gustavo Gutierrez's *A Theology of Liberation* appeared in 1973 (rev.edn, Maryknoll: Orbis,

1988), and was followed by a wave of liberation theology writing, much of it from Latin America. Rome has been ambiguous about it. Paul VI in *Evangelii Nuntiandi* in 1975, following the synod on evangelization, spoke at length affirmingly on the need for liberation (##29–39) and on small communities (#58), and subsequently John Paul II spoke similarly to the South American bishops at Puebla and Medellin. But the Congregation for the Doctrine of the Faith published in 1984 a quite negative *Instruction on Certain Aspects of the Theology of Liberation* neglecting the previous pontifical teaching, ignoring Jesus' programmatic statement in *Luke* 4, and treating of injustice not as the condition of people but as the consequences of sin. Following an intervention by the Brazilian bishops to the Pope, a further instruction followed in 1986, still very guarded and reluctant to condemn the conditions giving rise to liberation theology, even urging the poor and afflicted to "offer up" their sufferings (#47).

A helpful overview of feminist exegesis and theology is given by Katharine Doob Sakenfeld, "Feminist perspectives on Bible and Theology," *Interpretation* 42 (1988), 5–18. For some of the many other contemporary theological methods you might look at Neil Ormerod, *Introducing Contemporary Theologies. The What and Who of Theology Today*, Sydney: Dwyer, 1990, and J. J. Mueller, *What are They Saying about Theological Method?*, New York: Paulist, 1984. On the other hand, you would be advised first to acquire a basic grasp of theological processes, idioms and concepts before plunging into the reading of these quite difficult exponents of the science. Name-dropping is not a basic theological skill.

EXERCISES IN THEOLOGY

1. Depending on your artistic preferences (music, drama, painting), take a series of representations of one of the Christian mysteries (e.g., Incarnation, Trinity, Church) and comment on the theology of the artists for adequacy and impact.

2. Can you detect in yourself a maturing in the way you theologize— about God, about Jesus, about the Church, about the Bible, about life as a whole? To what do you attribute this theological growth— study, personal influence, life's experiences? Can you understand why people might retain a less developed style of theologizing?

3. If you have any doubts about the need for a feminist reading of the Bible, read chapters 19–20 of the book of Judges, one of the "texts of terror" Phyllis Trible offers her readers. Are the attitudes implied in the text a thing of the past?

13

Theology and religious education

"Making sense of faith" seems a rough and ready translation of St Anselm's brief definition of theology a millennium ago, *fides quaerens intellectum*. Aquinas would begin his *Summa* with an even more sublime definition, "a kind of share in God's own knowledge of himself." Any religious educator would be happy to have achieved that in the students, you would think, an understanding of faith and a share in divine knowledge. Provided, of course, the educator was thinking in terms of faith and not of religion, as the nominal definition of RE might suggest to some. Anselm and Aquinas did not have religion in mind. Which is it to be—faith education or religion education? We spent some time in Chapter 1 recommending beginners not to confuse the two.

The great medieval theologians, of course, did not have religion in mind in the sense of the great world religions. They knew only a little of Judaism and Islam and were unaware of the great religious developments in Asian religions even before Christianity's advent. For Aquinas *religio* is simply a virtue, as Karl Barth observes; it appears in the *Summa* under ethics (IIa-IIae, qq.81ff). Barth himself, a great modern Protestant systematizer, had no high esteem for religions, of which he should have had closer knowledge than his medieval counterpart. "We begin by stating," he says in his *Church Dogmatics*, "that religion is unbelief. It is a concern, indeed we must say it is the one great concern, of godless men."

FAITH AND LEARNING

We do not share Barth's view of religion and divine revelation as mutually exclusive; even Paul, Justin and Irenaeus would seem to have led us beyond that position. Nor, on the other hand, would we see "religious" education directing itself solely to a study of religion and world religions, as some would, partly on the grounds of the nominal definition, partly out of a false sense of faith as "fif"—a "funny inside feeling" beyond the reach and relevance of educational approaches. That, of course, is a travesty of faith as understood in Christian (and Jewish) tradition, as we saw in Chapter 1. That tradition likewise reinforces consistently the close link between faith and learning—from (the rabbis to) Irenaeus to Augustine to Anselm to Aquinas to Rahner and Lonergan and Macquarrie, if not the fundamentalists with their anti-intellectual attitude. We have only to glance at Anselm's objective in his *Fides quaerens intellectum* (later entitled *Proslogion*), cited on the dedication page of this volume. We need only listen to Augustine's urgent insistence in his Sermon 43, based on the plea of the equally insistent parent in *Mark* 9, "I believe; help my unbelief!", that his work as faith educator for his congregation works for the growth of the faith they already have in the revealed Word:

> Intellege ut credas; crede ut intellegas.
> *Understand with a view to faith; have faith with a view to understanding.*
> *I will explain in a nutshell how to take this without arousing controversy: Understand my word with a view to faith, have faith in God's Word with a view to understanding.*

Modern faith educators, too, are suspicious of attempts to divorce learning and faith education, as though religion alone were a proper object of education. Such attempts, often by people without an adequate understanding of faith, have been made to represent faith development as achievable only by some sort of osmosis within a faith-filled group; for them critical reflection on the faith does not and should not have a central place. Thomas Groome, whose shared praxis approach to religious education is by no means deprecatory of the role of the community in faith formation, sees the fallacy of those who would discourage critical reflection and the learning of which Anselm and Augustine spoke:

> *To do otherwise is to settle for a narrowly cognitivist epistemology that separates "knowing" from "being" instead of honoring an epistemic ontology as the foundation for education in Christian faith.*

> SHARED FAITH (1991), 194

We began with the admission that theology is not religious education; while both are conducted in the light of faith, they differ in their processes and objectives, their skills and idioms. Unless one takes the view that theologians should simply explicate defined doctrine, the critical reflection that is appropriate to theology, teasing out all the implications of positions held in faith, reconciling apparent contradictions and examining further possibilities (which further theological reflection may not confirm), is not appropriate for adults or children whose own acquaintance with the Tradition is incomplete. What religious education excels at doing is to apply all the skills and resources of good education to promote that basic acquaintance at various levels.

THEOLOGY'S COMMUNICATION PROBLEM

Communication, for instance, is not necessarily a characteristic of good theologians in whatever field of specialization. An exception to this herself, Mary C. Boys has to admit of one such group that "biblical scholars have an educational problem." Someone who has worked to adjust this educational deficiency, Eugene F. Trester, was prompted to do so by its urgency:

> *It becomes increasingly obvious that the wealth of knowledge currently available in the realm of biblical scholarship has somehow tragically failed to flow out into the lives and minds of adults.*

Anyone who has read the more philosophical of modern theologians, like Rahner and Lonergan, would agree that those who work in the area of dogmatics likewise do not always attempt to communicate readily with the theologically illiterate.

Hopefully educators will take the trouble to acquaint themselves with the findings of theological scholars in their work of seeking new ways of making sense of faith, and thus broaden their theological horizons in religious education. The vast array of critical approaches to the Bible listed in the previous chapter should have considerable impact on religious education in those communities for whom the Bible is the principal, if not sole, reference. Inadequacies in faith education spring not simply from scholars' lack of communication but also from educators' lack of contact with the fruits of scholarship. Biblical scholar Joseph A. Fitzmyer laments that "in Scripture matters, education today is so retrograde that one cannot even pose a critical question without shocking people."

What the scholars have to offer is also to suggest that people generally take advantage of advances in all areas of Christian tradition—not simply biblical tradition, but liturgical, doctrinal and moral traditions as well. Sacramental programs, for instance, have benefited much from theologians' fresh understanding of the meaning of sacrament and the practice of the early community in regard to initiation of new members. Family-centered, parish-based programs are becoming the norm, and the involvement of parents and the wider community has been a potent influence in their faith development, not simply the children's.

RELIGIOUS EDUCATION AND DOCTRINE

Keeping in touch with developments in the doctrinal tradition is also a responsibility for religious educators, particularly in those communities like the Catholic, in which that tradition is given a more pronounced role. For Catholic educators Vatican II redrew the boundaries and presented new challenges, such as an understanding of Church and the laity's role in it. The Council's sixteen documents have possibly yet to be plumbed and implications for faith education realized—such as the more positive attitude to other religions expressed in the Declaration *Nostra Aetate*. Magisterial statements from Rome have since then appeared with greater frequency; keeping in touch has called for added study.

In 1992 (1994 in English) a new *Catechism of the Catholic Church* was issued, "a compendium of faith and morals," the implications of which have also to be worked out in practice. Theologians and religious educators can work together in various ways on this latest task: determining the level of magisterial authority this new style of document enjoys; situating this catechism amongst others that have appeared since the Counter-Reformation; discerning the theology that informs its pages; and thus estimating the place it should occupy amongst the resources for RE today. In length alone it rivals the documents of Vatican II, but not in authority, being the work of a committee rather than a conciliar process. It is not intended for classroom use; rather, it is to be a "reference point" and model for producing local texts.

FAITH AND EXPERIENCE

While theologians make a contribution to faith education by constantly clarifying the traditions of the community, inviting educators to drink from the various founts, they should also remind them that a valid faith itself depends on our experience of God's word and action in Jesus. If we have not had that experience, our faith will be fragile. Young people and old are implying as much when they remark of the Christian Passover, "I get nothing out of it; it does nothing for me," and sometimes give up. Paul was able to speak validly for the community's value system in nominating what is "of first importance" after a lengthy period of experience of community traditions from Peter and others. But he had first enjoyed his Damascus experience, which certainly left an indelible impression on him, to judge from its frequent mention in *Acts* and *Galatians*.

That twofold formation is paradigmatic for us. For one thing, we need the insertion into the community's foundational experience that the traditions provide—biblical, liturgical, doctrinal, our lived experience of a good home and parish. It *is* a legitimate expectation that when the community celebrates the Christian Pasch, it will be a formative experience—which is not to say I will feel good about it; *experience* and *feelings* are not identical. But neither should it be sterile. Likewise, doctrinal processes in the community should not be heavy-handed but illuminating; adults at least who have been introduced to the sections in the new *Catechism* on the liturgy and prayer in particular, enriched with the abundant scriptural and patristic documentation that is a feature of the book, have warmed to the treatment. Doctrine does not have to be dull, and is not dull when presented by innovative, well-informed teachers.

But we each have our own life experiences, like Paul's on the way to Damascus, that are one way of God sharing himself with us in revelation. We meet people who mirror God to us. In Chapter 1 we recalled the deep impression made on a dying Hindu by Mother Teresa's self-sacrificing attention, prompting him to exclaim, "Glory to Jesus Christ through you." To the agnostic Malcolm Muggeridge, too, the same example proved to be *Something Beautiful for God,* in the title of the book he wrote about his transforming experience of her. A teacher who is in love with her subject, who is thoroughly committed to the Good News he brings to his pupils (little though they may admit it at the time), leaves an impression more profound and lasting than mere words; many of us have had that providential experience in our faith development. Learning theorists tell us that teachers pass on knowledge not simply through facts, or through knowledge of the explanatory frameworks that guide inquiry, or through knowledge of the way research brings new things to light. A key way to learning is through the teacher's beliefs and convictions about the subject in hand. "Were not our hearts burning within us while he was talking to us on the road, while he was opening the Scriptures to us?" (*Lk* 24.32). Religious educators, too, should be able to break the bread of the Word in such a fashion, thus providing unforgettable experiences for those growing in faith in other, perhaps more pedestrian ways. Small wonder the Fathers classed teaching as the art of arts and science of sciences.

SOME FURTHER READING

The debate on the nature and scope of religious education has continued for a long time since opportunities for school education became universal. The Bible, the Fathers and the medievals, though concerned for the ministry of the Word, did not lay the stress on the educational context to the extent that the current debate does. It could be said that today's educationists, by contrast, sometimes lack the theological depth of their forebears; and RE does involve some understanding of theological realities along with educational principles. That is why it is helpful to find in the one educator a combination of both, as in Thomas Groome; his *Shared Faith* (following his *Christian Religious Education*, 1980) appeared in 1991 (San Francisco: HarperCollins).

Groome and his colleague from Boston, Mary C. Boys, both having this experience and background in two fields, write well of the scholars' problems as educators and vice versa. They combined to write up lectures on the subject given to American educators in "Principles and pedagogy in biblical study," *Religious Education* 77 (1982), 486–507. Boys has written further on the topic in "Religious education and contemporary biblical scholarship," *Religious Education* 74 (1979), 182–97. Eugene F. Trester has concentrated on the faith formation of adults; taking his cue from Malcolm Knowles's principles for adult learning, he insists that good education of adults "will happen only when we shift the focus from the activity of the teacher, however qualified and gifted, and begin to refocus attention on the learners" ("Adult biblical learning in community," *Religious Education* 77 [1982], 542). He has devised a program of biblical study in small groups for adults known as ABIL (adult biblical interdependent learning), which is popular throughout the English-speaking world. I have surveyed the challenges and developments in biblical education at various levels in *Breaking the Bread of the Word. Principles of Teaching Scripture*, Rome: Pontifical Biblical Institute, 1991. My main hope is that the teachers will be well prepared in institutions catering for this preparation.

The impact of the new *Catechism* on religious education is still in the process of being examined, and the question has generated much attention in journals such as *The Living Light*. Addressed directly to bishops, at 800 pages it takes a committed adult to delve into it with guidance, and one who is capable of dealing with material that is abundantly documented rather than user-friendly. I have raised the question of its scope, purpose and use in "Catechism? compendium? reference? model?", *Word in Life* 41 (1993 No.4), 3–5. The wider question of the place of doctrine in religious education is discussed by John Thornhill in "Handing on the faith," *Word in Life* 35 (1987 No.2), 5–9.

EXERCISES IN THEOLOGY

1. Have you had the advantage of solid learning experiences in your faith formation? Did you find your faith responded in the way Augustine expected of his congregation'? Or do you lament the lack of solid learning about the faith?

2. Are you capable of making a judgment about the character of faith education these days, whether of young people or adults? Do you think there is a balanced accent on introduction to the community' traditions and the experiential element? What happens, in your experience, if the balance is upset?

3. Theology and religious education do not share identical processes or objectives; explain the differences. Is there a place for theological study in the course of faith formation? Under what conditions?

A theologian's resources

What prompts our faith, we have insisted frequently, is God's word and action—in Jesus, preeminently, in the case of Christian faith. We are enabled—with God's grace—to respond through our experience of that word and action, an experience that is immediate in the Damascus experiences in our life, and that is derivative in the ways we are inserted into the community's foundational experiences of Jesus through the various forms of transmission, or tradition. In our theologizing, when we endeavor to make sense of faith, we invoke and investigate all those traditional forms. The new *Catechism* warns us against "The Bible Alone" approach to theology (#108); it might equally warn us against "The *Catechism* Alone" or "Denzinger Alone" approach.

So at the basis of our theologizing lies the source of our faith. We bring to theology the richness or poverty of our faith and its share in those immediate and derivative experiences of God's word and action. Does it follow that the greatest theologians should be the most saintly? Perhaps so, especially if we accept Aquinas's definition of theology as "a kind of share of God's own knowledge of himself," and like Augustine in his work on the Trinity speak of our being ravished by desire for following up divine truth. Theology is a noble calling; after theology, in the words of the Thomistic commentator Cajetan, there is only the beatific vision.

HISTORY OF THE COMMUNITY THEOLOGIZING

Fortunately, for us lesser mortals, short of the beatific vision, there is available a range of resources assembled over time to help us tap into the community's traditions. We are not the first to endeavor to make sense of faith; and it is good for us to be aware of the efforts of our predecessors in the community. We might therefore begin by acquainting ourselves with the processes followed by these earlier believers in studying our various traditions. Source material is collected in historical collections like Henry Bettenson, *Documents of the Christian Church*, 2nd edn, New York: Oxford University Press, 1967; Lucien Deiss,

Springtime of the Liturgy, Collegeville: Liturgical Press, 1979; Robert Grant and David Tracy, *A Short History of the Interpretation of the Bible*, 2nd edn, Philadelphia: Fortress, 1984; and J. N. D. Kelly's books on early Christian creeds and doctrines, cited in earlier chapters.

BIBLICAL TRADITION

We have seen the emphasis given, sometimes exclusively, to our community's biblical tradition, *norma normans* as some would have it. Of all theological traditions, especially in modern times, the biblical has received the most voluminous attention, especially from Protestant scholars. Not all of us can deal with original texts in our theologizing; so we need access to a close translation (as distinct from one that settles for paraphrase in places, like the *Good News*, which nonetheless has its advantages in less academic situations). There is a wide range of sound translations, many recently revised; the preface by Bruce Metzger to the *New Revised Standard Version* (1989) sets out helpfully the principles of the revision, such as the stance adopted to sexist language and patriarchal biblical attitudes. For an evaluation of translations and of other biblical resources we need a bibliography such as that by Joseph A. Fitzmyer, *An Introductory Bibliography for the Study of Scripture*, 3rd edn, Rome: Biblicum, 1990.

Such a bibliography will take us through other helpful resources for theology. We will need an Introduction to the Bible, or to Old and/or New Testaments, giving us all the details about each individual book, like author, date, place of composition, content, current attitudes to intepretation, current literature—so there is nothing elementary about such "Introductions" (unlike a simple Guide for beginners, like my *The Scriptures Jesus Knew. A Guide to the Old Testament*). The range is wide. Earlier standard Introductions (usually by painstaking German scholars), like Otto Eissfeldt's *The Old Testament. An Introduction* (3rd edn, 1965) and W. G. Kümmel's *Introduction to the New Testament* (seventeen editions by 1973), have been matched by more recent English scholars, like Brevard Childs, *Introduction to the Old Testment as Scripture*, London: SCM, 1979, and Raymond F. Collins, *Introduction to the New Testament*, New York: Doubleday, 1983. A commentary differs from an Introduction in commenting on the text of a biblical book, verse by verse; there is a great range of them, including even *The New Jerome Biblical Commentary* (eds R. E. Brown, J. A. Fitzmyer, R. E. Murphy, Englewood Cliffs: Prentice Hall, 1990), which serves as both Introduction and commentary.

We may in our theologizing require even more information on the biblical text. A lexicon helps us with words in the biblical languages, whereas a Bible dictionary lists all other items of biblical interest, such as dress, seasons, personages and so on. There are also specifically theological dictionaries of the Bible, the most famous being that in 10 volumes on the New Testament edited by G. Kittel, *Theological Dictionary of the New Testament* (1933–79), Eng. trans. 1964–76, Grand Rapids: Eerdmans; Kittel will give you a thorough statement by a reputable scholar of, say, "faith" in Old and New Testaments and related literature. A concordance is of help in listing all occurrences of one word, like "faith," in one translation of the Bible. Naturally, the journals, at various levels of sophistication, will discuss issues bearing on theology to a degree; some we have cited in our "Some further reading" sections above so as to introduce you to them gently. And, of course, in this computer age, journals and other resources are indexed on CD-ROM, a resource not available to Anselm or Aquinas.

LITURGICAL TRADITION

One of the most valuable liturgical resources is, of course, the liturgy itself, celebration of the community's foundational experiences in *anamnesis*. While we can participate in our community's contemporary style of celebrating the mysteries, we may need documentary assistance for studying the communities East and West of other ages at worship. We may turn for this historical information to Deiss, or J. Martos, *Doors to the Sacred*, rev.edn, Tarrytown NY: Triumph Books, 1991; or Herman Wegman's *Christian Worship in East and West. A Study Guide to Liturgical History* (1976), Eng. trans., New York: Pueblo Publishing Co, 1985. For a general treatment of liturgy, a standard text is *The Church at Prayer*, ed. A. G. Martimort, 4 vols, rev.edn (1983), Eng. trans., Collegeville: The Liturgical Press, 1986–87, or Peter E. Fink, *The New Dictionary of Sacramental Worship*, Collegeville: Michael Glazier, 1990; C. Jones et al. (eds), *The Study of the Liturgy*, rev.edn, London: SPCK,

1992; or for the East Peter D. Day's *The Liturgical Dictionary of Eastern Christianity*, Collegeville: Michael Glazier, 1993. Catholic theologians will be interested in magisterial statements on the liturgy, which are collected by the International Commission on English in the Liturgy as *Documents on the Liturgy 1963–79: Conciliar, Papal and Curial Texts*. Another collection is *The Liturgy Documents: A Parish Resource*, produced in Chicago by Liturgy Training Publications and edited in successive editions by M. Simcoe and E. Hoffmann. Again the journals can be helpful; for beginners, *Worship* in the United States, *Liturgy News* from Australia.

DOCTRINAL TRADITION

Stating "What the Church teaches" has always been a challenge that theologians seem to have failed to respond to with the sort of simple directness that the questioner was expecting—though plenty of would-be theologians have been game enough to answer in a one-liner. Readers of the new *Catechism*, for instance, have been disappointed in its treatment of original sin, not so much for lack of directness this time as for mere repetition of Tridentine formulas now in need of refinement. Its treatment of faith likewise reverts in places to the Thomistic intellectualist view of Vatican I, whereas Vatican II (cf *DV* 5) made a vitally transforming contribution. The old *Catechism*, of course, had no qualms about one-liners; and we have been trying to undo the damage ever since.

A theologian versed in the history of the community theologizing should be able, in the manner of a Congar, De Lubac or Pannenberg, to trace the development of doctrines from the Bible through the Fathers East and West (in Chapter 5 we cited the modern translations of their works, available in a good theological library) to the medievals and into modern times. Manuals are to hand, however, which do that exercise for us beginners—though it perhaps involves some theological judgments by them on inclusion and exclusion.

If it is simply a matter of tracing the history of doctrinal statements at the level of conciliar or papal magisterium (which is not the community's whole doctrinal position, of course), we have the collection of Denzinger-Schönmetzer referred to before. Since it collects the statements in the language of the original, usually Latin or Greek, they are usually cited (e.g. in the *Catechism*) by the Denzinger number (DS) and then given in translation from the handy collection of Neuner and Dupuis, which we also introduced in Chapter 6. There are manuals and textbooks for every division and area of theology, varying in theological adequacy. Covering the whole range is a mammoth task attempted in a theological dictionary, such as J. A. Komonchak, M. Collins and D. Lane (eds), *New Dictionary of Theology*, Dublin: Gill and Macmillan, 1990. It is not a medieval-style summa; just a collection of entries on a huge range of theological topics. Richard McBrien classes his *Catholicism,* from which we have quoted, as "an attempt at a (Catholic) systematic theology"—all you ever wanted to know about theology but were afraid to ask. And, of course, there is an impressive array of theological journals, some of which we have cited.

******

This abundance of resources—biblical, liturgical, doctrinal—if daunting to a beginner in theology, is nonetheless both testimony to the industry of your predecessors and a wonderful bonus in your efforts to make sense of faith. Your faith should lead you on to seek understanding, as Augustine suggested to his congregation. But as well all your efforts at understanding are meant to develop faith. This text aims at nothing less.

Glossary

The **APOPHATIC** tradition in theology, as distinct from the KATAPHATIC, stresses what cannot be known (about God, for example), thus proceeding by way of negatives rather than by demonstration of positives.

ARCIC (Anglican-Roman Catholic International Commission), established in 1966 by Pope Paul VI and Archbishop Michael Ramsey of Canterbury, produced a series of joint statements collected in *The Final Report* (1981). ARCIC II has continued to meet.

BASILEIA is the word that appears constantly on Jesus' lips in the Greek New Testament (usually, but often unhappily, translated "kingdom"), meaning God's reign and value system that he comes to inaugurate.

CANON, a Greek word for yardstick or norm (cf Canon Law), is applied to that group of scriptural works found normative for a particular community, for example, Jews, Orthodox, Catholics, Protestants.

COMMUNION is from the Latin for sharing, fellowship, participation (Greek *koinonia*). It is used in a particular sense for sharing in the body and blood of the Lord.

COVENANT, or treaty or alliance (*testamentum* in Latin), is the word used in the Bible as a political figure for the relationship God forms with his people (as on Sinai) or with individuals like Noah and Abraham.

CRITICISM, from the Greek for "judge, evaluate," means, in biblical and general literary matters, evaluation of a piece of literature; so there is nothing negative about critical techniques (unlike English use of "critical" in other contexts), of which there are various kinds (see chs 9 and 12).

DEMYTHOLOGIZING is the process of distinguishing the MYTH, or figurative overlay, that in the course of time has been applied to a person or event highlighting its significance.

DOCETISM (from the Greek "to seem") in the early Church was an approach to the humanity of Jesus that questioned its reality.

DUALISM, from Lat. *duo*, "two," is a philosophical approach that tends to separate and even oppose what should rather be integrated, for example, spirit and matter, soul and body.

ECCLESIA is a Greek (and then Latin) word for Church. ECCLESIOLOGY is the study of the Church or ECCLESIAL matters.

ECUMENICAL, an adjective from Greek *oikoumene*, "the inhabited (lit. 'housed') part of the world" (Greek *oikos*, "house"), has the meaning "universal" (when applied to Church councils), or embracing all religious groups and not simply one's own.

EXEGESIS is the Greek term for explanation, applied especially to the Scriptures, a process in which the EXEGETE brings linguistic, historical and literary skills to bear on the text.

GNOSTIC sects, placing accent on the importance of special knowledge (Greek *gnosis*) independent of normal incarnational ways of coming to know God and find salvation, were known in the early Church, and mentioned in the New Testament and the Fathers.

HELLENISTIC, from the Greek word for "Greek," refers to the period and culture when Greek influence held sway in the biblical world.

HERMENEUTICS is the study of meaning and the ways to interpret biblical texts.

HYPOSTASIS is a Greek word which can mean person; so we speak of the HYPOSTATIC union by which in the person of Jesus divine and human natures are united. HYPOSTATIZATION (e.g., of the figure of Wisdom in biblical works) would therefore mean more than personification, a mere figure of speech.

IMMANENCE, from the Latin for "remaining within," is one of the divine attributes by which God is present within his world and not simply superior to it.

INCARNATIONAL theology stresses God's sacramental way of dealing with us so that spiritual goods come to us through tangible realities (Jesus, the Church, the Bible, the Eucharist, daily events, etc.).

KINGDOM, the usual (if inadequate) translation of *basileia* in the New Testament, is there less a geographical or political entity than the reign of God and his will and values that Jesus comes to inaugurate, in keeping with the Old Testament's picture of Yahweh as king.

KOINONIA, Greek for sharing, fellowship, participation, communion. The New Testament uses it of God's sharing life with us, and our sharing with others.

MAGISTERIUM, Latin for the office of teacher (*magister*), is applied to those who teach by right of office in the Church, especially (but not exclusively) pope and bishops (see ch. 10).

MANICHEISM, named after its founder Mani, was one of those dualistic (Latin *duo*, "two") sects in the early Christian centuries that set at odds two things that should rather be integrated, such as spirit and matter. Gnostic and docetic views were similarly dualistic.

A MODEL in theology, as in other sciences, is an image or analogy that has the capacity to assist in explanation of the whole reality (such as the servant model of Church, the model of Jesus as liberator).

ORTHODOX (literally, "having correct beliefs") is the name applied to Eastern Christians who are not in union with the patriarch of the Western, Roman see.

PASCHAL is the adjective from Hebrew *pesach*, Passover. The PASCHAL MYSTERY is therefore the great reality which is Jesus' death, resurrection, exaltation, celebrated at the Easter season of the Church's year.

PATRISTIC theology and literature come from the Fathers (Latin *patres*), those great spokesmen in the first eight centuries of the Christian Church, East and West (see ch. 5).

RABBI, "my great one," is a term not generally used until New Testament times, but this class of Jewish commentator and teacher arose in Old Testament times, producing oral Torah and the *midrashim* (see ch. 7).

SYNOPTIC (Greek "looking together") is the name applied to the Gospels of Matthew, Mark and Luke, who have a similar viewpoint on the life and ministry of Jesus by comparison with John.

The **TALMUD** is the collection of law and lore, including MISHNAH and MIDRASHIM, developed at the hands of rabbinic commentators for the community of Judaism in the period from the return from Exile into the Christian era (see ch. 7).

TaNaK is a mnemonic used by Jewish people of the Hebrew Bible, referring to its three major divisions: *Torah*, *Nebi'im* ("Prophets"), *Ketubim* ("Writings"). The Christian Old Testament is generally structured and named differently.

TRADITION (Latin *tradere*, "hand on") is the process by which the community hands on—through Scripture, in worship, by teaching, in catechesis and so on—its basic experiences. The term can also be used of the product of this process.

TRANSCENDENCE, as distinct from immanence, is that divine attribute by which God surpasses all human categories.

General Index

(Basic theological terms like *faith, religion, revelation, experience, tradition* occur repeatedly in the text and are not indexed here.)

Index of biblical citations

Index of modern authors